THE ART OF

Over 70 Gorgeous Macramé patterns + Projects Ideas

Callie Valdez

© **Copyright 2020 - All rights reserved.**

The content contained within this book may not be reproduced, duplicated or transmitted without direct written permission from the author or the publisher.

Under no circumstances will any blame or legal responsibility be held against the publisher, or author, for any damages, reparation, or monetary loss due to the information contained within this book. Either directly or indirectly.

Legal Notice:

This book is copyright protected. This book is only for personal use. You cannot amend, distribute, sell, use, quote or paraphrase any part, or the content within this book, without the consent of the author or publisher.

Disclaimer Notice:

Please note the information contained within this document is for educational and entertainment purposes only. All effort has been executed to present accurate, up to date, and reliable, complete information. No warranties of any kind are declared or implied. Readers acknowledge that the author is not engaging in the rendering of legal, financial, medical or professional advice. The content within this book has been derived from various sources. Please consult a licensed professional before attempting any techniques outlined in this book.

By reading this document, the reader agrees that under no circumstances is the author responsible for any losses, direct or indirect, which are incurred as a result of the use of information contained within this document, including, but not limited to, errors, omissions, or inaccuracies.

Table of Contents

Introduction 5

Chapter 1: Macramé- An Overview 6

    1.1 Terms Used In Macramé: 10

    1.2 Macramé materials 12

    1.3 Material Preparation 14

    1.4 Basic Knots 14

Chapter 2: Macramé Patterns: Decorative Items 18

    2.1 Macramé Christmas Tree: 18

    2.2 Simple Macramé Table Runner DIY 21

    2.3 Macramé Keychain With Tassels 34

    2.4 Frog Holder 38

    2.5 Macramé a Tea Cup 56

    2.6 Tree Decoration 69

Chapter 3: Macramé Patterns - Daily Use Items 85

    3.1 Hammock Chair 85

    3.2 Macramé a Basket 96

    3.3 Designer Hat 101

    3.4 Macramé Pillow 110

    3.5 Window Belt 116

    3.6 Shopping Bag 126

Chapter 4: Macramé Patterns-Latest Decoration Ideas ... 145

    4.1   Macramé Rose 145

    4.2   DIY Macramé Feathers: 165

4.3	**DIY Macramé Mason Jars**	170
Chapter 5: Macramé Pattern: Fashion Item		176
5.1 Striped Clutch		176
Conclusion		192

Introduction

This book is a detailed list of over 30 macramé knots and designs, plus some creations. Learn how to make over 30 macramé knots and tiny designs, then use them to create a large variety of projects. Within the book you can see illustrations of each knot, with easy step-by- step diagrams demonstrating how they are tied. Beginning with the simplest, the knots go on to more intricate and complex patterns, but it is still easy to understand because all of them are diagrammed. The essential guide opens with a description of various terms used in Macramé, the various types of available threads or cords, some basic knots and then some interesting patterns. This book contains valuable knowledge such as setting up the workboard, among other helpful tips such as keeping track of the ends of the chord for less ambiguity. The designs range from basic pieces such as decorative ornaments, and key chains to more complicated ones such as a number of bags and baskets. This book is an excellent guide for fresh and more experienced knotters both.

Chapter 1: Macramé- An Overview

Handicrafts were always a very fundamental human activity; for, crafts are an integral part of human life. Few crafts such as macramé can prove to be fascinatingly absorbent and flexible. With the textile industry changing rapidly, there is a need to revive and replace the old craft into modern ways in this ever-changing market for newer fashion.

In old times Knots and knot lore were closely associated with magic, medication, religious views for much of history. Knots also acted as bases for mathematical structures (for example, by the Mayans), before writing skills were introduced; and string games and other alternate uses were and are still numerous, of course. All these things have been carried out in one way or another and by all races since ancient times. They are even being taught all over the world nowadays. Additionally, it is safe to say that it will continue to follow until the day comes that humankind no longer exists.

Macramé as an aspect of decorative knots permeates nearly every culture, but within those cultures, it can manifest in different directions. The carefully braided strings, with the assistance of a needle-like tool, became the item for shaping fishnets. Their use in the fashion industry has been spectacular and influential among the youth in making sandals, shoes, jewelry, etc. It is now used also with other products to fashion all kinds of beautiful works of art.

Macramé is closely associated with the trendy youth due to its rapid growth, quick adaptability, and extensive uses. Concerning its use for fashion items, macramé exercised in the textiles became an essential focus on the creation of each decorative piece of clothing, particularly on the fringes of each tent, clothing, and towel. In this, macramé became a synonym for hanging planter. In its traditional forms, Macramé (is an Italian name given in Genoa-its home and place of birth) became one of the most common textile techniques.

Knots are used for the passage of time for several practical, mnemonic and superstitious reasons. Knotting dates back to early Egyptian civilization in Africa, where knots were used in fishnet and decorative fringes. The Peruvian Incas used a Quip, made from mnemonic knot (Basically, overhand knots) to help them record and convey information. The use of ties, the knot size, rope color, and knot both helped to communicate complicated messages Knots were used in surgery (as slings for broken bones) and in games in ancient Greece (one such mystery was the Gordian knot). In the early Egyptians and Greek times,' Hercules ' knot (square knot) was used on clothes, jewelry, and pottery, which had a spiritual or religious meaning.

The near association between contemporary crafts and macramé has led to the discovery of a range of methodologies and integrative methods, common in most cases, in the content and the adapted techniques. Such advanced methods and integrative techniques reflect the accomplishment of macramé art and its development.

 As a product of the artistic intervention of scholarly artisans, this human intellectual accomplishment became necessary to incorporate modern architecture requiring the use of other materials for trendy artifacts. While macramé art has been created and used for onward creation in most cultures aimed at achieving both practical and artistic appeal, their end products vary from one culture to the next. These innovations, however, are, by definition, integral parts of cultural growth and are the results of the macramé artisans ' revolutionary accomplishments over the years. The use of adornment knotting distinguishes early cultures and reflected intelligence creation. It is an art that fits all ages and abilities. Today, macramé is experiencing a Revival of the 20th century. Both men and women transition to work with their hands and build not just utilitarian pieces but also decorative ones.

This simplicity and durability, given the importance of macramé, portrays macramé as just a kind of knotting technique, an off-loom commodity described from a non-economic viewpoint due to its slow production design. Macramé as a technique is full of vitality, adaptable, and exploratory and in several respects in product creation and production lends itself for processing and handling. Macramé painting has been a highly valued talent from the earliest times around the world.

The journey of macramé production, traveled through Arabia in the 13th century, Turkey, and Spain during the Moorish conquest, spread to the rest of Europe as early as the 14th century arrived
in Italy and France in the early 14th and 15th centurie
s and was later introduced to England in
the late 17th century and the mid-
19th century in the Victorian era.

Sailors and seafaring people
are said to have spread this art style all over the worl
d according to tradition.
By the 1920s, macramé had reached its dormant perio
d in China and America, making artifacts such as
flower hangers, skillfully made
boxes, and industrial containers.

Macramé has also proven to be an excellent natural treatment for those undergoing recovery procedures and helps to restore memories once again, making it a unique experience for all. Playing with and tying the ropes, strengthens arms and hands, which helps relax wrist and finger joints. It also helps to calm the mind and soul, as attention is necessary, and the repeated patterns put the weaver in a meditative mood. It is believed that stress is reduced by the fingertips, making macramé knotting a calming task.
Macramé has the added benefit of embracing the self-expression cycle by establishing the underlying purpose concealed within.

1.1 Terms Used In Macramé:

As you work on different Macramé patterns, you may come across words, abbreviations, and methods used in instructions like filler cords, cord holding, fusing, project board, etc.
Here is a list of some simple macramé words which y ou need to learn as you follow trends.

- Row: A line of knots write next to one another, each bound with a separate working rope.

- Alternating Cords: Forming a new set of cords by t aking a slice of the cords from previously

attached parallel knots, and joining the layers below and above where the cords start.
- Change Cords: Changing the position of braiding and filler cords to make the last braiding cords the filler cords and the last filler cords the braiding cords, respectively.
- Filler Cords: string in the middle of the knotting cords.
- Fusing: Fusion is done with Polypropylene. The process of joining two cords. Hold a lighter butane flame near the ropes, to melt together the fibers. The ends roll between the fingertips. (Wet your fingers to avoid being burned).
- Holding Cord: It's one of the most common terms used in Macramé. Holding cord is used to identify one or more cords holding and supporting the knots produced by active cords.
- Knotting board: It is usually a printed grid fiberboard. It can be used as a clipboard as well, or even a firm pillow, to hold your project up.
- Wrapping Cord: Cord used to gather a group of cords and tie them. You can see this on a plant hanger's top.
- Knotting Cord: the left and right strings used to form knots over filler cords.

- Picot: Loops created by stretching the active cords past the knot a length and then pulling them up to the knot above.

- Sinnet: A vertical series of knots bound continuously together, made from the same knot with the same working cords.
- T-pins: Metal pins that have a T shaped head. T-pin is used to attach your work to the Knotting Board. To add sturdiness, place the pins at an angle.
- Working Cords: All cords in a pattern, those doing the binding (knotting cords), and those wrapped around (filler cords).

1.2 Macramé materials

There are several recognized fabrics used to do macramé. These include silk, rayon, raffia threads, shoe sewing threads, cotton threads, jute, cloth strips, leather strips, shoelace, and all other lightweights, malleable, foldable, and durable and hand safe fabrics. Yet jute, silk, linen, and cotton are the most common fabrics used for Macramé as they tie easily, come in several sizes, can be dyed, and are readily available. Any yarns come with a wax, creosote, or scale finish on them. Besides, any material is suitable for macramé, which can be bought in incredible lengths and seems to be pliable. Jute, raffia, cotton, and rayon threads are indigenous to the materials described above.

- **Macramé Cord: Linen**

Linen cording comes in a broad range of colors and sizes that make it highly desirable for many styles of braiding. Linen does have the durability and range that most other cording materials don't have, making it ideal for Macramé projects which need to be sturdy and robust. Linen cording is mostly used in wall hangings in Macramé and looks fantastic when paired with other cording types, such as cotton and silk. The one thing to keep in mind while Macramé with linen cording is that it will unravel very quickly, so one needs to be very sure to finish the project's ends cautiously.

- **Macramé Cord: Cotton**

Cotton threads are weaker than jute, hemp, or linen and need more bending to allow them to hold together to form a chain. In most fabric and sewing shops, where you work, you can purchase cotton cording or even from weaving suppliers. Single-ply cotton is used for Macramé creations that you'll wear, like a shirt. Cotton cording tends to come in a wide range of sizes and is found in many designs of Macramé.
Where the finished piece would be used isan essential factor when selecting the form of cord for your projec t? Is it going to be indoors like a plant hanger? Then

you would need something that is fade proof. Are you making a hammock? You will need material that is soft to the touch.

1.3 Material Preparation

The supplies are not complicated to plan. It begins with product layout, which is desirable for the design and manufacturing process, then by choosing and selecting the color and material depending on the product to be produced and its quality and style. The design processes are critical since it mostly depends on the result of a full macramé product. At this point, the color pattern, purpose, and target market for the finished item are decided, followed by cord measuring according to requirement, clipping, cord mounting, knotting techniques, product decoration, and finishing.

1.4 Basic Knots

- **Square Knot and Half Knot:**

Two half-knots make up a square knot. Follow the instructions mentioned below to create a square knot. Start with the first four loose cords on the holding thread.

a. Take the outer left (knotting) cord and bring it in an L form between the two middle (knot-bearing) cords. At the end of the L put cord four on top of cord 1.
b. Then take the cord that is at the extreme right (4) below cords 2 and 3. Drag cord four upward through the opening between cords 1 and 2. You'll get a half-knot.
c. Bring the cord 1 back over cords 3 and 2 to complete the square knot. Layer cord 4 above cord 1.
d. Now put cord 4 below cord 2 and cord 3. Pull cord 4 over the space between cords 3 and 1. Pull the cords firmly up against the first half of the knot. You've got a knot in square done.

To prevent a lopsided knot, make sure that the knot-bearing cords undergo an equivalent amount of tension when pulling knots in place.

- **Alternating Square Knot:**

You will need eight cords to tie an alternating square knot pattern.

a. Join each set of four cords with one square knot, one knot opposite the other.
b. Using the following four cords, tie the second set of square knots: 3 and 4 from square knot to the left, and 1 and 2 from the square knot to the right.

Create another square knot using 4 and 1 for the knot bearing strings, and knotting strands using 2 and 3. The square knot in the top row will connect the cords beneath the two square ties.

- **Half-hitch Knot:**

A half-hitch knot produces a pattern just like a raised rib. According to the preference, it can be tied from the right or the left. Two cords are required to create a half-hitch, a knotting cord (1), and a knot-bearing cord (2). Place the knotting cord usually over the top of the knot-bearing cord. Then loop cord 1 behind cord 2 and down. Pull up on a knot-bearing cord before you reach the desired pressure.

Chapter 2: Macramé Patterns: Decorative Items

Decorating your home is the dream of everyone. The inclusion of decorative items will really make your house look amazing and stylish. The right decoration items will bring together all the components of your interior decor. One of the ways to decoate your walls with beautiful art is through Macrame. Macramé helps to create decorative items of versatile designs

2.1 Macramé Christmas Tree:

The macramé Christmas Tree Design is perfect for decorating your house, and it also makes a very good present. The piece's finished size will be around 31 inches in length, so pick a beautiful place on to the room wall to display the beauty!

Materials Required:

- 30, 20mm round redwood bead
- 7 ply 8mm of jute 41 yds in length.
- One dowel stick, 1.5" diameter 17" in length.
- One average sized bow tie and other ornament
- 1,1%" diameter ring or circle

Directions:

1. Cut fourteen strings of length 2 1/2 yds all.

2. Now cut two more ties. Their measures should be 3 yds both.

3. Wrap two of the 2 1/2 yds strings on the one and a half inch ring by the help of Lark's Head knots (LHK).

4. Move down to seventeen inches and wrap cords using Double Half Hitch knot (DHH) ties near the edge of the dowel.

5. Fold the two of three yards string. Strings in half now join 1 on every one of the external strings with Lark's Heads, near the top portion. Double Half Hitch (DHH) these tied strings to the inner ones.

6. Add one bead to two of your middle strings closest to the top edge, and then add one Square Knot (SK) underneath the bead with the help of the remaining four cords.

7. Wrap 2 two and a half yd strings, one on every exterior strings, with the help of a Lark's Heads knot (LHK), roughly an inch from the previous Lark's Head knot (as in step 3), now Double Half Hitch (DHH) these to the inner strings as you have already done in stage 3.

8. Split strings into two sets: each group must have four wires. Two middle-cords are your filler cords (FC) of every group. Take the two of your filler cords (FC) from each set and slide a bead through it, and make one square knot (SK) under every bead.

9. Join 2 more strings, as done in the last step, on the external cords, and Double Half Hitch (DHH) it all to the underside of the ties as done earlier.

10. Split the cords among three sections, four wires in each section, and repeat as done in step no 6, but this time with three beads.

11. Attach two more strings as set out in phase no 7.

12. Split the cords into four sets, of four strings in each set, and redo as in stage 6 with four beads.

13. Take down about an inches and make up four Square Knots (SK) in a line.

14. Redo stage 7 by attaching two more cords to the existing set. Now split these cords into five groups of four ties each, and redo as is done in stage no 6, but with five beads this time.

15. Again redo stage 7 by adding two more cords to the existing group; split ties into six groups and redo as is

done in stage 6. Redo this stage another time, the final time using seven beads.

16. Double Half hitch (DHH) all the cords to the rod of the dowel and put one bead at the ends of the dowel.

17. Collect all the cords and tie them up using a bow at about four inches underneath the dowel stick. Embed decoration into the bow, if necessary.

2.2 Simple Macramé Table Runner DIY

Consider them as layers which complement and contrasts when decorating any location. Whether it's color, shape, or size, these three elements will make a space feel less simple. The fourth piece of advice is on versatility! This Macramé table runner marks all the check boxes, and with its simple yet unique style has made this sleek breakfast nook much more unique.

All that is required to learn are three easy knots, and you have a charming table decoration at your hands. If you're aware with the knots mentioned here, then you can tailor your table runner that suits your table length, or alter it entirely and build a DIY wall hanging!

Materials Needed:

- 12 inch dowel
- twenty two strands of 16 inch cotton rope of length 3mm
- Scissors
- Over door handle
- 2 inch of cotton twine for the dowel hanger

Knots Used:
- the lark's head knot
- the half-hitch knot
- the square knot

Step by Step Instructions:

1. Tie cotton string to both the corners of your wooden dowel and suspend it using your over the door handle. Fold in half your 1st 16 inch rope loop, and build the head knot of a lark over your dowel. For more specific measures, please see this below.

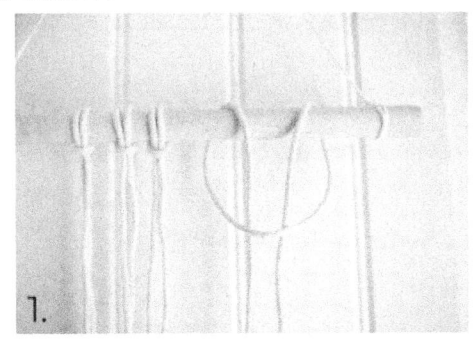

2. Continue to add up every 16' rope strand; use the head knot of a lark till you have a minimum of 22. That will send you 44 working strands.

3. Pull the right outer rope over the front side of all of your other ropes (to your left) and cover the end on the hook at your entrance. This will be the basis for the following row of knots called a half hitch knot which creates a straight row using the 2nd rope to tie a solo knot across the cord that you've just stretched over so that it's about 6" below your dowel.

4. Bind a second knot over the base strand using the same strand. This is considered a knot semi-hitch.

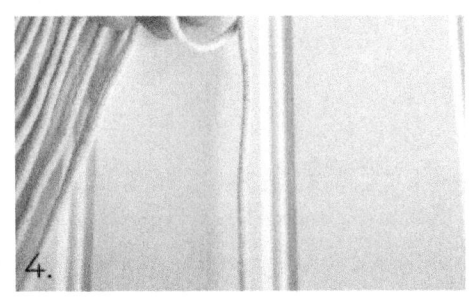

5. Assure they are clear and even.

6. Repeat from the outside with the 2nd, 3rd, and 4th rope and add a new half hitch knot to keep it tight, etc. You're going to start looking at trends. That is a Half-Hitch horizontal.

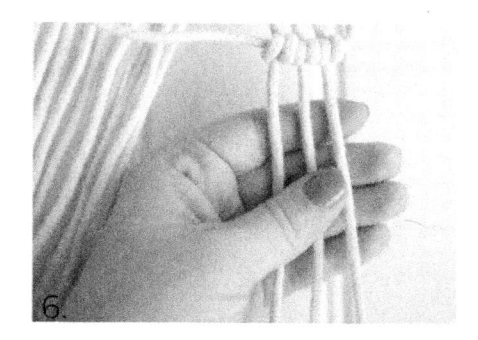

7. Continue to tie consecutive knots all around. Don't make this too close that the space at the sides is drawn in.

8. Using the outer four strands from your right side again, and make a square knot (SK) about 1.5" below the horizontal knots.

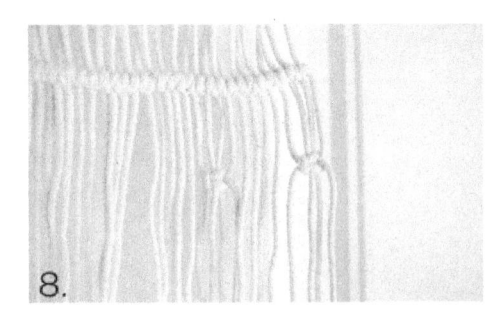

Miss the next 4 strands (five to eight) and use cords 9 through 12 to form another square knot. Start to skip four, linking up to four before you get through the whole way.

9. Using the 4 cords you missed (five to eight) and make a square knot (SK) around 3" under the dowel, beginning from the right side again.

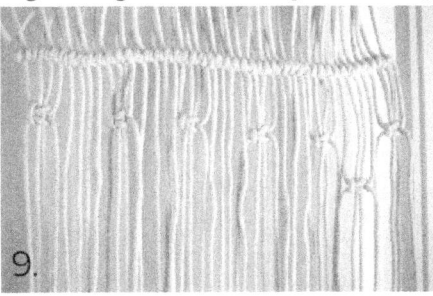

10. Keep ting the four- skipped sets in square knots (SK) until you end the sequence.

10.

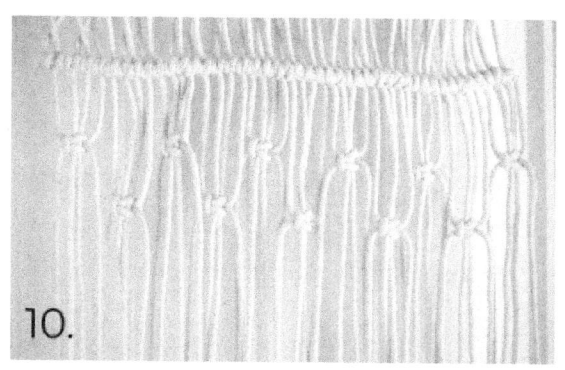

11. Move the two outer strands off to your left at the top. In step seven, we are using strands 3 to 6 to make another square knot (SK) about 11" below the horizontal row of knots. Then use the next four strands to construct another square knot over the last square knot (SK), around 1.5".

12. Go all around, as shown. With the past two lines, you won't do anything.

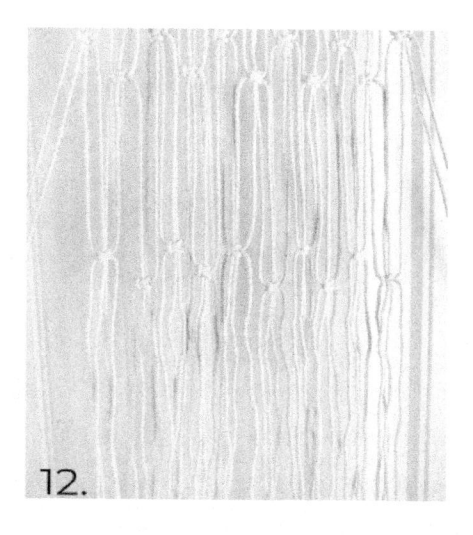

12.

13. Creates another series of straight half hitch knots beginning from the right side again by redoing phases from 3 through 7.

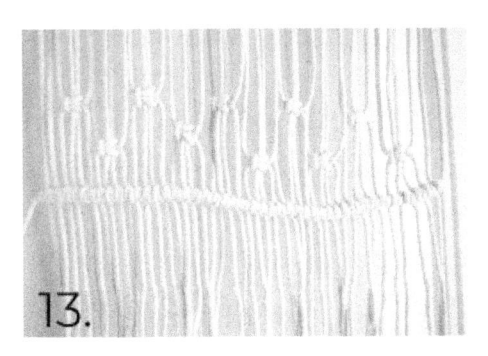

14. Using the similar base string of cord from the left side, then build a new horizontal half hitch line of knots about two and a half inch below the previous. On this one, you are going to be starting from left to right.

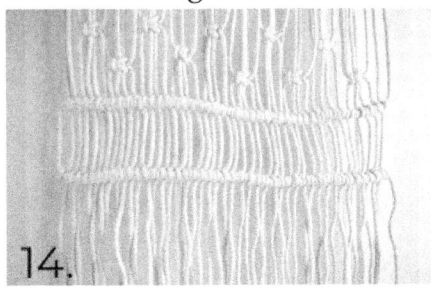

15. Build a line of square knots (SK) on the left side without missing any threads that lie around 1"

below the horizontal row of knot. Now make a 2nd row of square knots (SK) by missing the 1st two threads on to the left before joining a complete line of square knots together. This is known as alternating square knot (ASK). You don't want a lot of space between those rows, and you can draw them together closely as every square knot (SK) is applied.

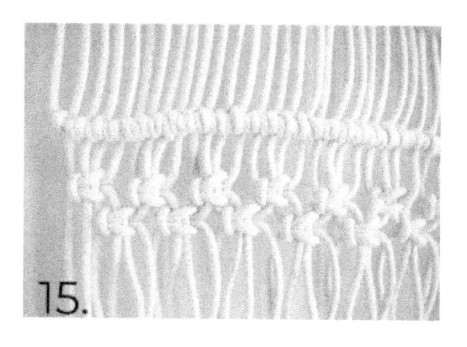

16. Redo until you have a limit of about thirteen rows of alternating square knots (ASK). This portion is the core of the table runner, and anything other after this stage should echo what you've already woven above.

17. Attach another half-hitch horizontal line of knots beginning from the outer left hand side and making the way to your right hand side.

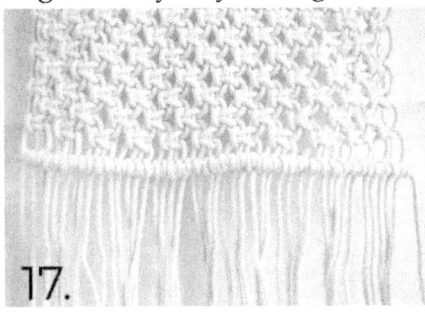

18. Dropdown another 2.5" and use the identical base rope to make another half-hitch horizontal line of knots going from right to left.

19. Miss the outermost 2 strands of the rope to the right for this part, and now tie a square knot (SK) by taking strands 3 to 6. Miss strands from seven to ten, then use strands from 11 to 14 to make a new square knot. Undo, so for every 4 strands, you missed. On to the left hand side, you will have six strings.

Miss 1 and 2 cords on the left hand side and tie three to six strands to make a square knot (SK) approximately 1.5" below the last row of square knots. Then miss the next 4 strands and end the pattern for the square knots second section. This would put you on the right hand side, with six extra strands.

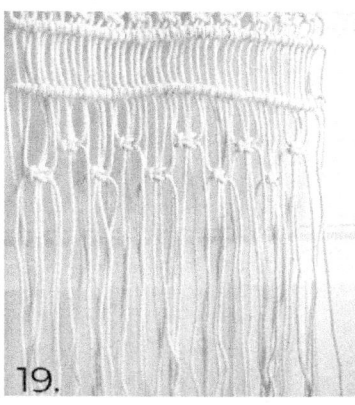

19.

20. Measure 11" from the last created line of horizontal ties and make a square knot (SK) to the right using the four outer threads. Then tie the following 4 cords into a square knot (SK) over the previous knot, around 1.5".

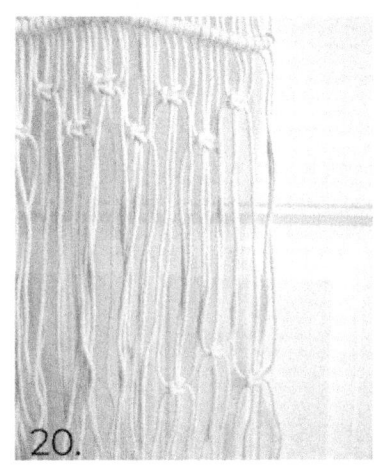

21. Repeat the same, entire way

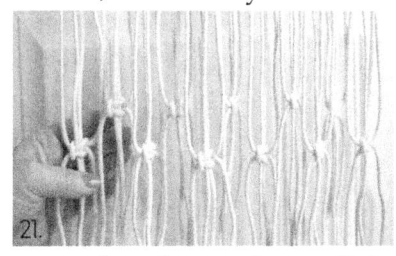

22. Lastly, tie one last line of parallel half hitch knots around 1.5" under the alternating square knots (ASK) level. Trim the edges to be as lengthy as you wish, indicating how lengthy they are on the differing end. Clip the cotton string from the dowel and softly pull off all the knots of the lark's head. Now cut the head knot core of the lark, and shorten the ends.

Your table runner's center is the right place for a decoration, so put on a vase, and finds some fresh roses to support anchor your eye. You may also use it on a breakfast slab as your own giant place mat to ensure your kitchen looks its finest! You may also use the 3 basic knots you've mastered, the lark head knot (LHK), the half hitch knot and the square knot (SK) to make a number of layered wall hangings!

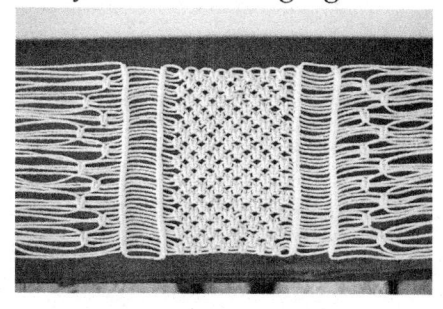

2.3 Macramé Keychain With Tassels

Materials Needed:

- A Empty Key Ring
- Cotton strings
- Beads 3 of 16 inches
- Yarn Or any embroidery floss
- Tiny Rubber Band only for key chain no 4
- Scissors

Step By Step Instruction:

KEYCHAINS USING SQUARE KNOTS (SK)

Let's begin with keychain no 1 (above) and keychain 6 (below).

They're created with a basic square knot (SK) and the half square knot (HSK), its incomplete but stylish sister.

- For both the key rings, you'll begin with 2 fifty inch or so pieces of string. Pass each through the key ring with a larkspur (LPK) knot, making the outside strings about 2/3 the length of original cord.
- For keychain no 1, create about 5 square knots (SK), add bead, add a half square knot (HSK) below it, and bond the rest off into a fringe.
- Create about 16 half square knots for key chain # 6, and end with a tassel.
- Use your favorite embroidery thread colors to give your tassel the ideal fancy neck.
- Separate the ends of the cord, cut it down, and you're done!

Useful tip: Press the bottom down to snap off the tassel's bottom exactly straight, and cover it with sheet of tape. Break the adhesive tape in two, take it away and rejoice at the great fringe.

Macramé Key chains With Ornamental Beads And Fringes

Use the same strategy for key chains no 3 (to the left) and no 5 (above) but vary the amount of beads and the size of the fringe.

- For both of the two, you will begin by adding a 10-16" portion of yarn with the help of larkspur knot to your key ring.

- Attach the beads.

- Split yarn for the fringe-we used approximately 20 yarn pieces. (Cut it double the size of your tassel). Align it in the center-right under your bead and join it with a simple knot. Now tighten the tassel and the bead, and double the simple knot.

- Bend the fringe in half and tie a thread or any embroidery floss around the neck.

- Chop the ends. That is it!

Macramé Keychain (Chk) Striped Clove Hitch (Sch)

Key chain no 2 (above) that looks complex but fancy — but it takes only two simple knots to create the trendy, personalized color palette.

- Begin with 2 of 20" parts of cord (you can still cut them short, but starting long is better). Loop through with a larkspur knot (LPK) through the key ring, creating the outside threads a little bit longer than the inside
- Ones — add perpendicular clove hitch stitches with some few different yarn colors. We've

done two rows in the 1st two colors each, and 1 row in the 3rd.
- Create a Square knot (SK) in the center.
- Connect a third group of perpendicular clove hitches (VCH), but opposite to what you did on top end.
- This finishes off with a short trim at the ends.

MACRAME KEYCHAIN WITH A FOLDED BRAID

Key chain no 4 (above) is incredibly simple to make.
- Cut 3 parts of cord just more than double the size you like for the customized keychain finished.

- Pile them, level the threads, and tie one end a little below the other, with a tight rubber band.

- Do just one braid. End until the rubber band is equidistance from the ends as you are.

- Loop one of the ends through the key chain. Place the rubber band about the two ends to keep them in their place if you wish.

- Begin the neck from underneath your braid. (You should break the rubber band free when you start covering the neck with some of your embroidery floss).

2.4 Frog Holder

Your custom Frog Holder has a cute green frog hooked to a mettle ring (or a branch). It looks he is using his big webbed feet to carry the ring. You may use some beads for his eyes, but it is suggested that you seek to find plastic eyes, that has stems and some washers preferably.

Like the eyes seen in the illustration below the finished height of the frog is around sixteen inches, starting from the top of the frogs eyes down to the ring bottom.
This Macramé project is Easy, so it is very appropriate for beginners.

Materials Required:

- 6mm green color cord material at least 56 yards

- Two 25mm an inch Frog Eyes or tiny bead
- Two 1.5 inch metal Rings
- 7 inch Ring or a 12 inch Branch
- Crafting Wire
- Project board, Glue, and pins

Knots Used:

- Double Half Hitch (DHH)
- Overhand Knot (OHK)
- Vertical Half Hitch (VHH)
- Alternating Square Knot (ASK)
- Reverse Larks Head Knot (RLHK)
- Square Knot (left and right both)
-

Step By Step Instructions:

1. Cut fourteen strings, each four yards in length. Prepare the ends for preventing unraveling when you are working on the Frog Holder.

2. Attach a four yard cord with a reverse Larks Head knot to the top end of your ring by folding the string in half and installing it at the top of your ring. The edge will go to the back side of the Project Board. Take the edges below the ring then above the cord's folded region, going up towards you.

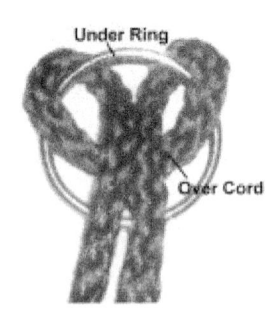

3. Slide one on both parts of the cord if you decide to use **bead**s for your Frog Holder's eyes.
4. Wait before all the strings are attached to place a plastic Frog eye (Step 4).

Use a Double Half Hitch to connect every end of your rope to the lower edge of the ring (a solo Half Hitch is seen in the picture below — ensure you added two). Ensure you pull tightly on the string, so the region within your ring has a lot of tension.

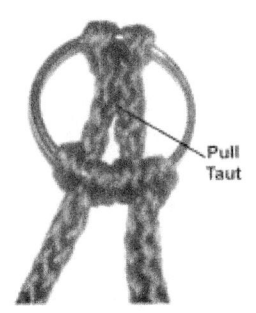

5. Join another cord with the help of Reverse Larks Head Knot (RLHK) on the right side of your ring.

Ensure that the folded region heads external to the ring. This would be reverse of the last one, which headed to inside of your ring.

Make one Half Hitch Knot (HHK) into the ring with each edge of the latest cord, lying next to your Larks Head knot (LHK).
The illustration depicts the ring position.

Join one more string in the same way on the right hand side of the ring. Join two more strings on the ring's left-hand side. This gives you a sum of five new cords connected to your ring.

Put the stem of one of the eye right through the first cord's two sections (in the middle of the ring).

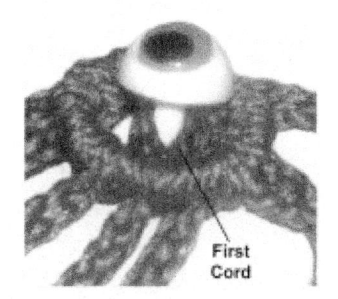

Move the ring over, so you are operational at the back.

Attach the washer into the stem. Ensure it is forced as far as it is possible inward.

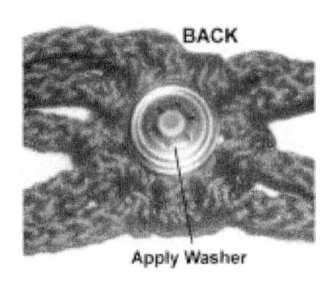

Apply Washer

6. Redo steps 2-4 to build your Frog Holder's second eye model.

7. Now place the 2 rings next to each other, leaving a little space for yourself to work. The ten strings on each circle are mentally labeled (from left to the right). Using 9 -10 **cords** from the left side ring together with **1-2 cords** from the right side ring form a Square Knot (SK). Transfer the rings back together when tightening (see illustration below).

8. Attach an Extra Square Knot from the extra ring with strings 7 to 10. Stiffly twist it until it lies near the 1st knot made in stage 6. Attach a Right Square Knot from the right ring using cords 1 to 4. (See underneath)

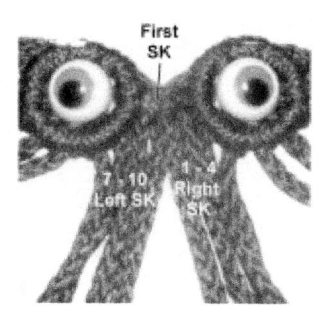

When you tie a right Square Knot, you start by curving the appropriate working string. That is cord 4, in your case.

You start for a left Square Knot with the working cord (WC) on the left side.

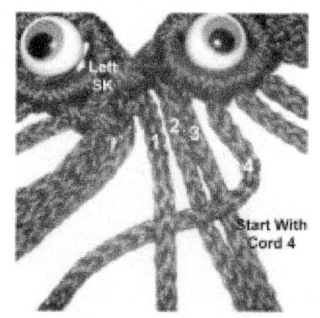

Useful tip: Adjusting the orientation of the ties will make sure all sides of your Frog Holder are symmetrical.

9. To create row no 3, mentally mark all strings from left to the right. Tie a Left Square Knot using the following cords 1 to 4, 5 to 8, and 9 to 12. Attach Right Square Knot using the following cords 13 to 16, and 17 to 20.

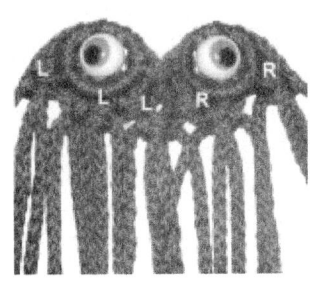

10. Tie Left Square Knot to continue row 4 with the help of cords 3 to 6 and 7 to 10. Connect Right Square Knot by using the cords 11 to 14 and 15 to 18

11. Attach 1 cord to Frog Holder's left hand side by bending it in half now slip it under your cords one and cord two. You are using two halves of your newly attached cord to tie a Left Square Knot. The fillers are strings one and two.

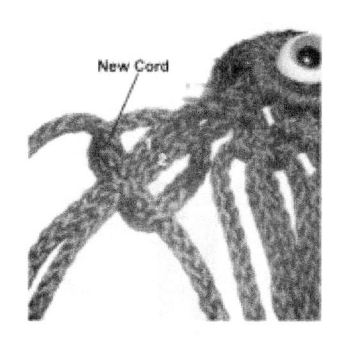

12. Attach 1 string to the right hand side by bending it in half now slip it between nineteen and twenty strings.
    Tie a Right Square Knot using the newly added cord. The Fillers are cords nineteen and twenty. Re-number all the cords mentally from 1-24.

13. To start row five, tie left square knot using the cords 3 to 6, 7 to 10 and 11 to 14.

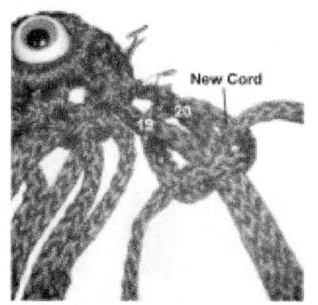

    Using cords 15 to 18 and 19 to 22 tie a RIGHT Square Knot.

14. Redo stage 10; use a LEFT Square Knot to attach another cord to existing cords one and two.

Redo step 11, use a RIGHT SK to attach a new string to the cords no twenty three and twenty four.

15. Re-number all the cords mentally from 1 to 28. For your row no 6, join Left Square Knot with 3 to 6, 7 to 10 cords, and 11 to 14 cords. Make a RIGHT Square Knot with the help of cords 15 to 18, 19 to 22, and 23 to 26.

16. For row no 7, tie a left square knot using the following cords 5 to 8, 9 to 12, and 13 to 16. Attach Right Square Knot with the cords 17 to 20 and 21 to 24.

17. In this region of your Frog Holder, the final row is secured as follows: Tie Left Square Knot with the cords 7 to 10 and 11 to 14. Attach Right Square Knot with the help of cords 15 to 18 and 19 to 22.

18. Switch string one to the right side, to use the mouth of the Frog Holder as a holding cable. Keep it secure, so that it has some tension. Attach 2-14 cords with a Double Half Hitch in a counter-clockwise direction to it, securing each one tightly. Switch the holding cord (HC) according to your Square Knots curve.

Switch cord no 28 to the left side, to use as the right holding cable.

In that order, add cords 27 to 15 to the holding cord with DHH in a clockwise direction.

19. Combine your holding cords one and twenty eight with fourteen and fifteen, then make one Square Knot (SK). Remark all the strings, mentally. For making the lower lip of the Frog Holder; shift cord one to the right side, to remain being used as your holding cord.

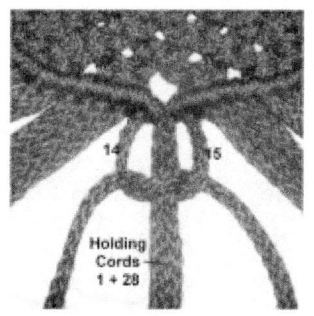

Connect 2-5 cords of DHH **counter-clockwise** to it, pulling every cord tightly such that the 2 rows are close to one another.

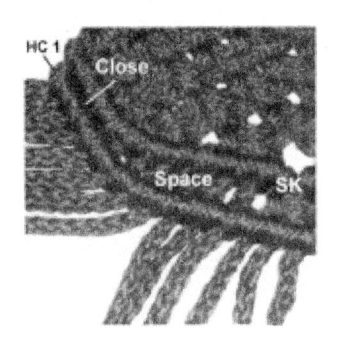

Add cords 6 to 14, slowly increasing the gap between the 2 DHH rows. The DHH will settle against the Square Knot before you hit the middle, so tie the knots tightly and move them as closely together if required.

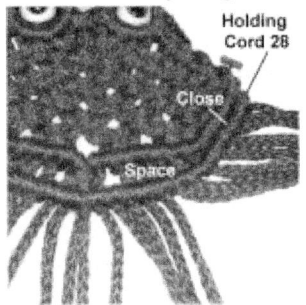

For using a cord as your holding cord shift cord no 28 to the left. Connect cords 27 to 24 to DHH in a clockwise direction, so that the 2 rows are near one another.

Now fasten cords 23 to 15 on the left with the similar width as the bottom lip. As you continue, bring the ties closer together.

20. Re mark the strings, mentally. Cords from 9 to 20 are taken to shape the Frog Holder's body. Join 7 ASK rows as mentioned below: Rows no 1, 3, 5 and

7: Add Left Square Knot with cords 9 to 12 and 13 to 16; Tie RIGHT Square Knot with cords 17 to 20.
For rows no 2, 4 and 6: tie Left Square Knot with cords 11 to 14 and a RIGHT Square Knot with cords 15 to 18.

21. Now you're going to make your Frog Holder's front feet.
Attach a nine Square knots snit using 5 and 8 cords. As you advance, bring the knots closer together.

Useful Tip: Make sure between the First Square Knot and the Double Half Hitch there is no gap. The sennit lies at an angle, heading outwards. They curve as the limbs are connected to your ring.
Repeat this step with the help of cords 21 to 24. Position the 7 inch ring or your branch in the frame against SK's last row. In the position next to the body, the front limbs will be touching the ring (see picture below). If required add additional knots.

22. Place the cord no 7 (left side leg) below the loop, then fasten it with a Double Half Hitch. Cord no 8 is to rest near the figure. Do the similar with a cord no 22 (your right leg), pin it to the right side. Cord no 21 is expected to be near body.

23. Cut 1 piece of wire, at least 25 inches long, to begin the left sides back leg for the Frog Holder. Pass it through the cord 2 Double Half Hitch (left mouth side), and bend it in half.

24. Create an 18 Square Knot snit with one and four working strings. Your fillers are 2 and 3 cords (and both the splits of the wire).

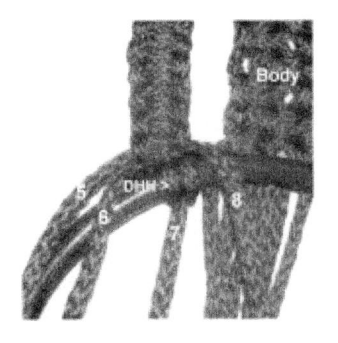

25. Cut another piece of 25-inch wire and slip it into DHH created using cord no 27 (right section of the frog's mouth).

26. Connect an 18 Square Knot senate with the twenty five and twenty eight operating cords. Have the cords as a filler portion.

27. Go back into the left side front leg of frog and position five, six, and eight cords at the top of your ring. They will be the holding cords for the frog's foot, so hold them with a little tension.

28. The first six body cords from 9 to 14 are the working cords for the foot. Be sure that both the limb and figure fit close together.

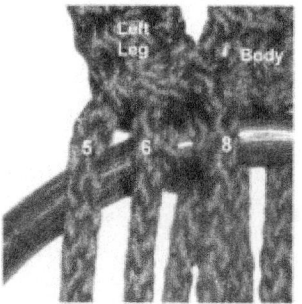

29. Move you're working cord no 9 under your ring, and under your holding cord no 8 (from the frog's leg).

30. Tie a Vertical Double Half Hitch into cord 8, turning in the counter-clockwise direction, so that the cord still goes right to the left.

31. The 2nd knot rests right below the 1st while rendering Double Half Hitch vertically (seen on the picture below). Move cord 9 below cord 6, then tie the next vertical Double Half Hitch. Move cord 9 below cord 5, then tie the last DHH.
All three ties will rest next to each other.

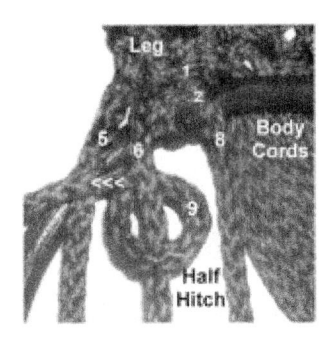

32. Repeat stage 26 with 10-14 working cords, to create additional Vertical DHH rows.
Increase the distance between your knots after you tie each row by pushing your holding cords farther apart.

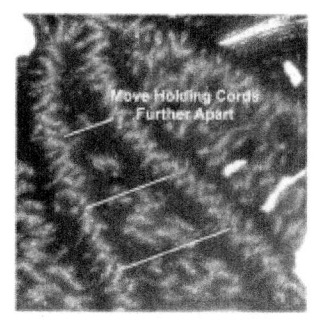

33. Finish your holding cords by applying an Overhand knot (OK) to each, placing it next to the previous DHH string.

    Apply glue when tightening. When it's completely dry, take off the excess product.

    You should add heat to the stubs when using Bonnie Braid to melt your tiny stubs.

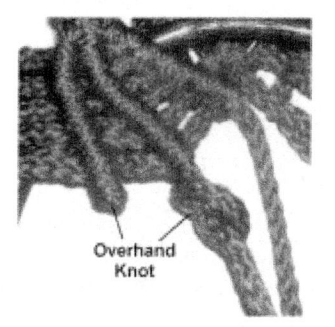

34. Redo steps 25 to 28 to get the front foot right. We are using Square Knot sennit strings 21, 23 and 24 (right side leg), as holding cords.

    You are using 20-15 body cords (in the same order) to connect the Vertical DHH line. The Half Hitches (HH) are connected in a row in the clockwise direction, as you pass from left to your right.

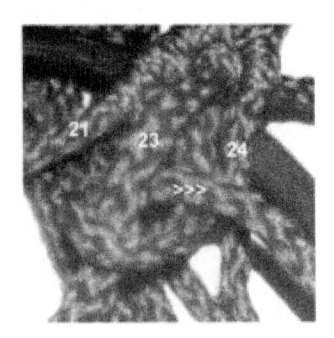

35. Bow the left leg back to the place where the Square Knot 6th and 7th lies necessarily.

36. Test to ensure that the sennit with the limb bent enters the loop. Make extra Square Knot if needed.
    Wrap the wire around it and add the limb to the ring. Join one of the strings to it too. Start wrapping the Double Half Hitch around the cable, one coil on each leg.
    Slip the knot around the opposite side.

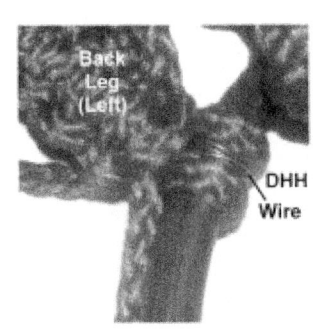

37. Place the remaining three cords on the top of your ring from the back leg so that it is used as cord holders.

38. Build the webbed foot as you created in steps from 26 to 28, by using same front-foot working cords (body cords 9 to 14).

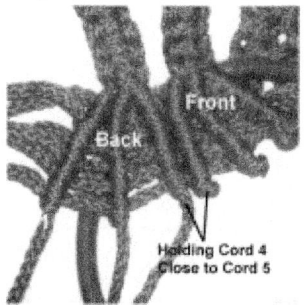

Useful tip: The Frog Holder's feet look better when they're close to one another. So place carrying cord 4 from the front foot next to cord 5, and tightly secure the Vertical DHH until there's no room between them. Redo stage 30 to 31 to add the ring to the right side back leg to build the feet.

Holding cord no 24 (front feet) will rest next to holding cord no 25 (back feet), so between them, there is not at all room. Using the same front-face working cords (body cords 20 to 15).

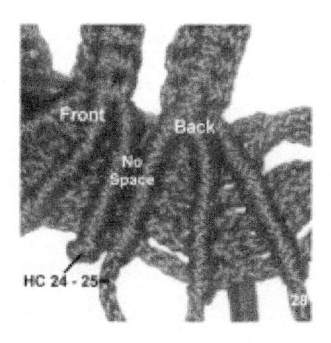

39. Switch your Frog Holder over, and you operate at the back side. Join working cords with DHH from the foot to your ring. This step is not mandatory, but it will provide your ring with better support.

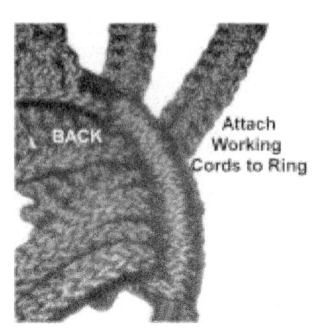

End of the strings by tying Overhand knots (OK) with groups of two strings. Add glue at the ends and snap off any excess material. When creating things with Bonnie Braid, you can heat the tips with a flame as well.

2.5 Macramé a Tea Cup

This Tea Cups Ornament is an amazing way to accessorize your kitchen. Put either real or fake roses, air fresheners, or other little objects inside the cup. The final dimension of the cup is 6 "wide and three inch tall.

To build together the cup and the plate, which is different in color, alternating square knots are used. These directions do not include the phases to tie a Square Knot (SK), so please make sure you know how to tie a square knot, or you can view it from previous chapters.

This project is classified as Easy, so it is perfect for beginners. Useful tip: Polypropylene or Nylon that can be melted as a part of the completing phase will be the material used to create this Macramé decor. Test the stuff by heating the material up. Don't use if the material will burns, instead of melting.

Materials Needed:

- Synthetic material cord that melts on heating 4mm in width
- 3 total rings: 1 two inch, 1 four inch, and one 6 inches in width
- Pin, project board, covering tape
- Lighter

Knots used:

- Square Knot (SK)
- Double Half Hitch (DHH)
- Alternating Square Knots (ASK)
- Overhand knot (OK)
- Larks Head knot (LHK)

Cutting Instructions:

- Use two different color cords color marked A for your cup and color B for the saucer.
- Color A: Cut twenty four cords, each twenty five inches in length (63.5cm in length).
- Color B: Cut twenty four cords, each twenty five inches in length.

Prepare the strings to create the Cup by adding the hiding tape to the edges or Overhand knots (OK).

Step by Step Instructions:

1. Wrap one of the Color A string (for the cup) with the help of a Larks Head knot (LHK) to the 4-inch ring: Bend the string in half and put it underneath the 4 inch ring. Take the edge above the ring and underneath the folded section.

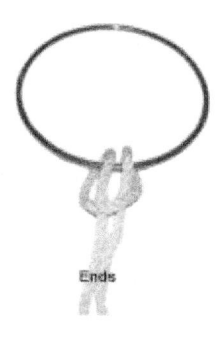

With each end make a Half Hitch (HH), by creating a circle over and under your ring. It will move over the cord as you pull on to the end in downwards direction.

2. Redo step 1 for all the Color A strings remaining.

3. For creating the cup, tie an entire row of Square Knots (SK) using a group of four strings.
   Tighten your knots tightly so that they sit as close as possible to your ring.

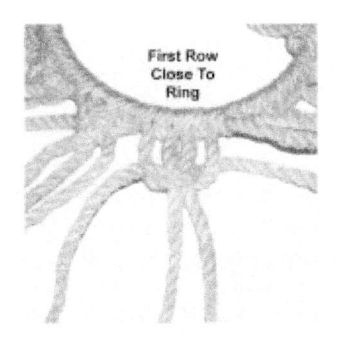

4. Wrap five additional rows of Alternating Square knots (ASK) to create the mug portion of your Tea Cup Decoration with color A cords.

5. For a rundown on how you switch cords, read the text below.
Useful tip: The ring has to be a tip or suspended with the help of something, so you're creating a small cylinder rather than a plane shape. See snapshot for step no 5.
The easiest way to alternate when constructing ASK is to imaginably list the cords that come from the two knots of the end row you that you tied. In the next row, merge cords three and four from the knot on the left side with cords one and two from the one on the right side, and use all of them to make the ASK.

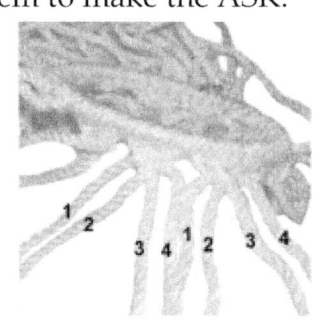

6. Attach one more line of alternating square knots. Move the Fillers to the inside of the cup,

and out the top portion, after each knot is tied. Just the working cords (WC) are connected to the new ring. To hold the fillers in to a group, use a rubber band any tape.

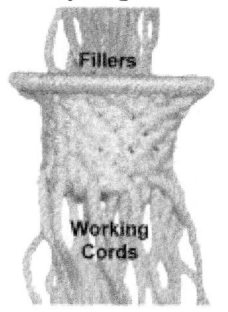

7. Attach twelve of your Color B strings onto your 2 inch new ring for the saucer. Connect them with the help of Larks Head knot (LHK).

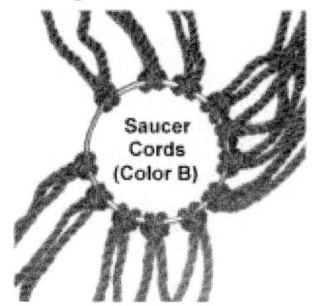

8. Slide all the working cords (WC) of your cup through the 2-inch ring as well. Position half of the cords of color B on the right side of your cup and the remaining on the opposite side.

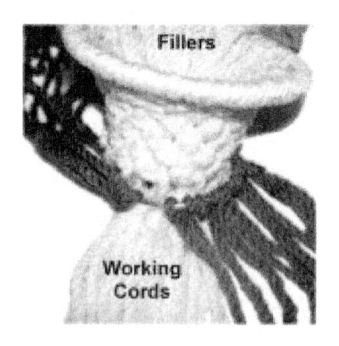

9. Add two cords with a Double Half Hitch knot in a counter-clockwise direction from the cup, as you should move from left to your right.

10. Slide a cord of Color B next to your two cords that you have just connected (from your cup). Now join two more Color A string by using Double Half Hitch knots to the ring.
Continue this same designs (two Color A -- one Color B), all the around your ring.

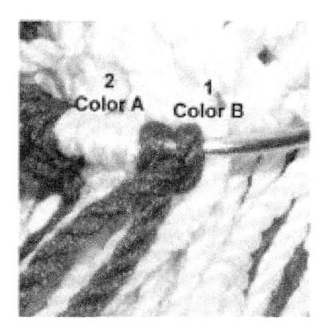

11. Invert your Tea Cup ornament and set it on the top end of the cup. Tie off each couple of your Color A string with tight Overhand Knots that you just added to the ring. Try to organize the ties so that they can settle within the ring, but not straight on the steel (see next snapshot).

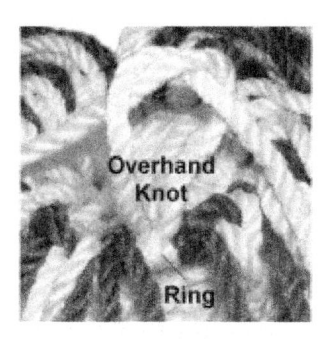

12. Snap off the extra material near every knot, but leave two very small tips roughly 1 by 8 of an inch in length.
Use a matchstick to heat the tips and melt

them so that they adhere to the tie.

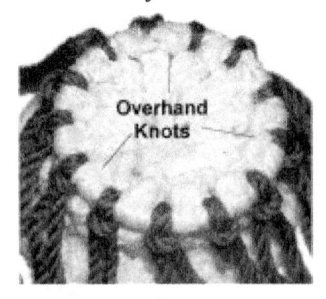

13. Trim the cords of fillers you put inside your cup to 1-inch, then unravel each to create a comfortable nest.

14. This won't stop heavyweight items from slipping through your ring. If you require a safe bottom, use a different finishing technique.

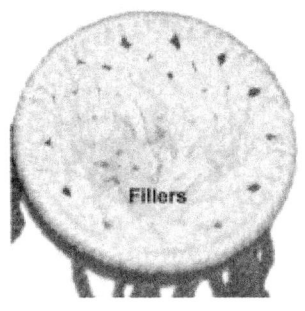

15. You must attach the leftover Color B strings to those on your 2 inch ring to create the saucer: Fold a new string in half and place it under 2 cords that are coming from your ring.   Use the latest added cord to create a Square Knot (SK).

The fillers are the cords that come from your ring.

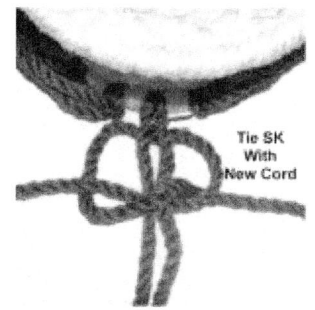

16. Now tie four rows of your Alternating Square Knots (ASK) after all the cords are connected.

17. Useful Tip: This is the utmost difficult step, so carefully tie every knot. The ties must stay flat on the work surface.
Too much tightening up the knots will make it to curl upwards. If that occurs, loosen the tie a little.

18. Attach every cord with a Double Half Hitches knot to your 6 inch ring. If needed, make extra Half Hitches (HH) to fully cover the ring.

19. You make the knots in a clockwise direction as you move from right to left. If you're going from left to your right, switch them to the counter-clockwise direction.

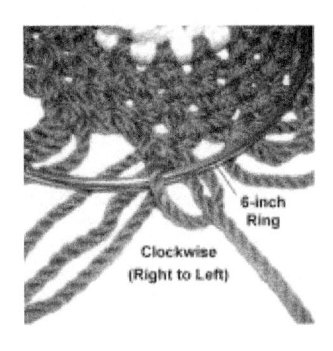

20. Snap off the cords ends by tying an Overhand knots with the group of two cords. Keep in mind to push your knots, so it stays to the inside of your ring rather than on top of it. Trim off the excess below you added knot, now heat up and melt the ends, as you did in step no 12.

21. Cut two of the cords, each thirty six inches in length (1 yard in length), to create the handle for the Tea Cup. Fix the tips using tape.
Push a few knots away to create space for the latest cords, at the top of your cup. Roll all of them under your ring, placed in such

a way that 6 to 8 inches head away from yourself, and the remaining dangle down toward your saucer.

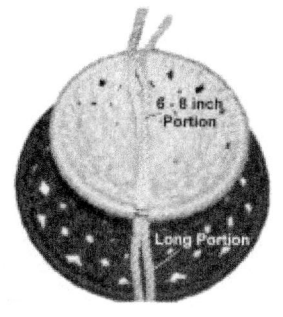

22. Passing on top of the ring, push the short segments towards you.

23. To add a Square Knot (SK) round the short parts, that are the fillers, use the long segments.

24. Pull firmly onto the filler strings (short segments) after the first knot is tied.

Tie some additional Square Knots, till your seniti is at least 3.5 inches in length.

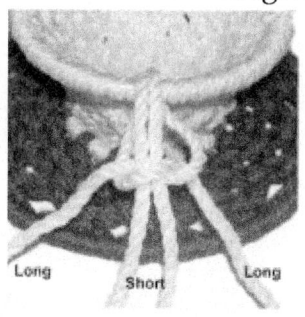

25. Roll all four handle cords, just above the 2-inch ring, into the gap at the lower edge of your cup.

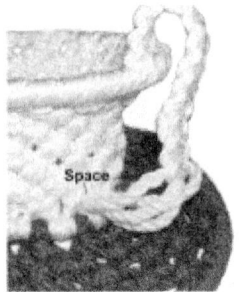

26. Flip your Tea Cup upside down now find the four handle cords.

    By using all four cords together, make one big Overhand Knot (OK). Trim the edges near the knot. Give heat and then melt the tips as you did before.

    Add flowers to the inside of your cup, potpourri, or similar items.

2.6 Tree Decoration

This Tree Decoration perfect to learn the Wrapped Knot (WK).

Cotton yarn is used to cover the ring, and to create the twigs and fringes inner base.

In some places use Jute or Hemp to make those places fully brown. Wrapped Knots (WK) can be difficult to wrap, especially if the ties are long. Before pursuing this design, learners should exercise ting a wrapped knot.

Materials Needed:

- Artificial vines with leaves or flowers
- 2mm Jute or Hemp -- for twigs (100 yards long)
- One 2-inch ring
- 3mm Hemp, Cotton, or Jute for the core and ring (100 yards)

- Project Board and pins
- One ring with width of 15 inch
- Medical clamps or pliers
- Craft wire (12 inches)

Knots Used:

- Wrapped Knot (WK)
- Reverse Larks Head Knot (RLHK)
- Double Half Hitch (DHH)
- Overhand Knot (OK)

Step By Step Instruction:

1. Join the 2 inch ring to your 15 inch ring by multiple times winding the cable around the two. Ensure the bond is strong and the narrow ring is not sliding through.

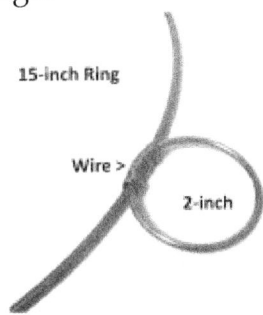

2. Cut a string measuring 3 mm, ten yards long. Put its center on top of the cable which connects both rings.
   Using both half to cover the 15 "ring in reverse

directions. Cover securely, and ensure there is no overlapping between the coils.

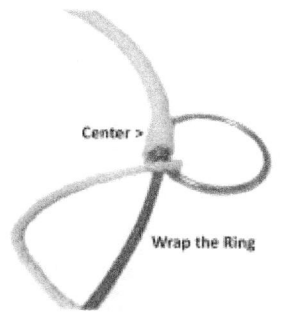

Center >

Wrap the Ring

When you advance, move the coils tightly together and there are no spaces. At the lower edge of the circle, the two ends will cross, straight down from the place you began (middle). End by knotting 1 or 2 Half Hitches to every half of your cord across the ring. Add glue before pressing.

3. Now it's the stage for your Tree Decoration to create the first branch. You begin by attaching the strings which make up the branch's Base (inside).

4. The ring was tied in a Cotton cord in the illustration given, and the center of the twigs is constructed from using same material. Brown fiber is Jute, woven around the middle.

Cut two cords of 3 mm thickness, each at least sixty inches in length. Mark the tips with Knots Overhand, or using tape.

5. Fold a cord in half now put it on top of your 15 inch ring close the 2 inch ring region.
   The fold would head for the inside of your ring.

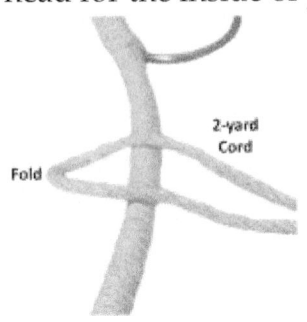

Move the edges under your ring and over the folded region of the rope, to complete the Larks Head knot (LHK). Drag the knot around the 2 inch loop, now pull the edges to secure it.

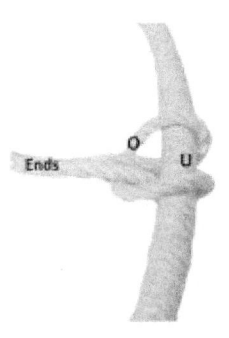

6. Repeat stage four using the other string, placing it next to the first one.

7. The 1st branch for your Tree Decoration is rendered using both cords.

2 Cords = 1 Branch

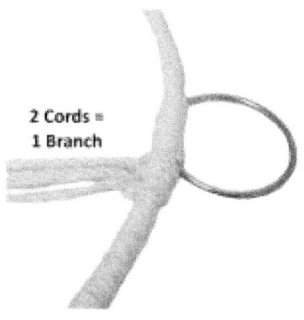

8. Cut one 2 mm working cord (Jute or Hemp) four yards long. Place the big circle on your work surface, so that your 2 inch ring is at the very top. At one end of your working chord tie an Overhand Knot. Place the tie between the holding strings on to the outer side of the 15 inch circle. Protect the knot by a pin to the work surface.

9. Measure 7.5 inches down from your ring, and then put a pin at that same spot.

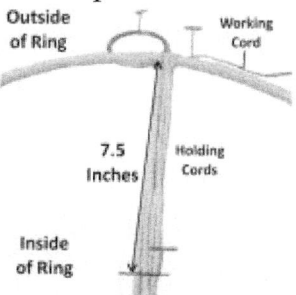

Outside of Ring / Working Cord / 7.5 Inches / Holding Cords / Inside of Ring

Bring down your working cord (WC) to your pin, then bend it and bring it back up to your circular ring. Take the extended portion of your working cord and move it out many times

73

through the palm. Take away the ball, and hold the bundle using a hair tie.

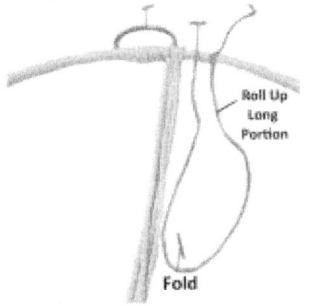

Roll Up Long Portion

Fold

Tie the working end round the base, as well as the held part of the working cord (WC). Cover securely, but NOT strongly, and move the coils closely together so no holes exist.

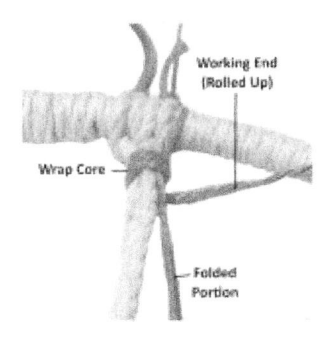

Working End (Rolled Up)

Wrap Core

Folded Portion

Useful Tip: The tension of the working cords (WC) in the brown material is very critical for effectively producing the Tree Decoration.

While wrapping the initial collection of branches, care must be taken not to cover too firmly, so that the wrapped part will slip. The working cord (WC) will fit round the base snugly, without needing to compact certain cords. You have to tie securely as you connect the twigs to one another and build the trunk so that the curls are clear.

Stop enfolding when you're past the operating cord's folded field (about 7 inches). Move the edge through the bent part, looking like a circle.

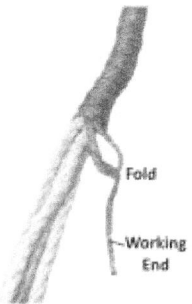

10. Go up to your ring and pin away from the protected edge. Remove it slowly by using the medical clamp (or tweezers).

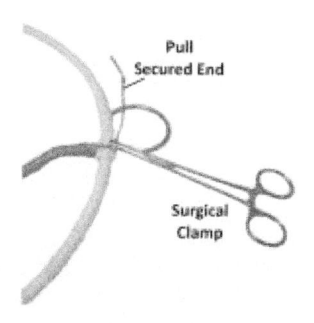

Within the Wrapped Knot is pushed the folded part   and   the   working   end.

Important: Pull firmly on every cord that makes up the branch's CORE. That will allow the branch to curve, which will make your Tree Decoration appear real.

Snap off the secured end of your working cord (WC), so that it is even with the top edge of the small branch (near your ring). Fold the stub within the enclosed part of the branch.
Do not break off the bottom of the surplus material.

11. Create at least ten more branches to decorate your tree, by redoing steps from 3 to 9. Distance between branches should be at least half an inch.

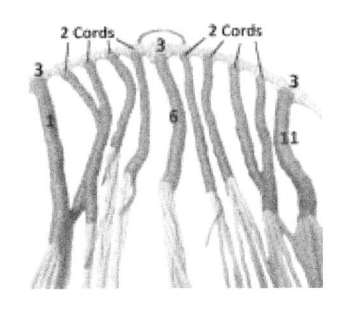

When making branch no 6, use either three or four holding cords (HC) for CORE that are at the center where the small ring is connected.

It makes the branch denser than any other branches. Your brown working cord (WC) should be at least five yards in length, so your branch should be 7 to 8 inches in length. Redo this step when creating branches one and eleven which are farthest left and right. If a branch is longer it improves the design. The remaining tiny branches should have different lengths for the Tree Decoration. When changing sizes, snap off the brown working cords down to the lengths below.

- 4 yards is equal to 7 inches
- 4.5 yards is equal to 7.5 inches
- 5 yards is equal to 8 inches

When measuring the size in step no 7, add half inches to the end branch height, then position the 2nd pin at that level.

Therefore the pin will be positioned 8.5 inches from your ring for an 8 inch branch.
Now you continue your Tree Decoration building cycle by joining the branches. Number them mentally from 1-11.

Identify twigs one, six, and eleven. These are the dense twigs for the core, consisting of 3 and 4 strings. These 3 branches will be known as "group 1"

12. Snap off 1 working cord, about two yards long. Bend branches six and eleven together, so that they appear natural. You may attach them next to each other or with 1 above the other. Bend 3.5 inches from one of the edge of the working cord as you continue to make the Wrapped Knot (WK). Begin the knot, at least 1 by 4th of an inch over the end, in the wrapped zone of the branches.

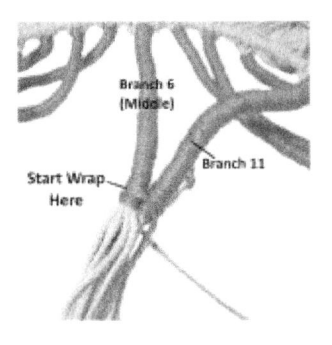

1-inch tie, meaning the cords are firmly bound to all ends, so that they all are as secure as likely. Take quite some time to link the branches, as neatness is very important.

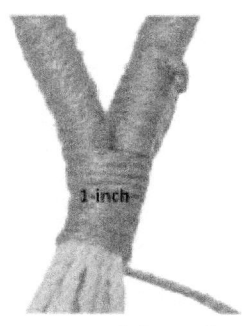

Useful Tip: When attaching the branches for your Tree Decoration, it won't be possible to shove the cords tight together.

So cover carefully, putting each coil under the preceding one, tightly fitting them. Eliminate any holes, so none of the cotton strings are reveled.

13. Place the branch one on top (or next to) of the two that you just attached to. Ensure the branch 1 bottom is at least half inch below the part where you ended wrapping in the preceding stage.

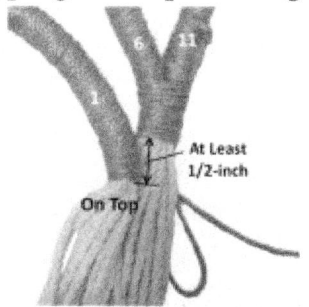

Start wrapping around on all 3 branches, for about 2 inches. End the knot by moving the end (as in stage 8) through the folded region. Pull the retained end (as you did in stage 9).

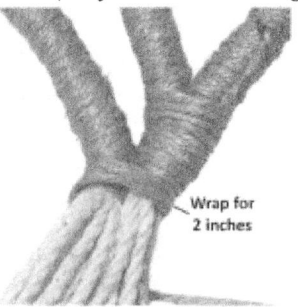

Wrap for 2 inches

14. Redo steps 11 to 12 joining four branches to create GROUP 2. Split the working cord (WC) at minimum 2.5 yards in length, because you have an additional branch. The knot Wrapped would be about 3.5 inches in thickness.

Useful Tip: Ensure you take the twigs on the circle from various places and link them in order to make your Tree Decoration appear as real as possible. Replicate the same procedure again to create GROUP 3, but split the working chord by at least three yards. This Wrapped Knot (WK) will be longer (at least four inches) than the other two types.

15. Now this is the time to attach all three chord categories, creating the trunk for decorating your Tree. They are attached to one Wrapped Knot which must be extensive enough to touch the ring's bottom end center area.

Identify group 1 from the three groups which is the 1st set of connected branches. Count the difference between the bottom of the ring and the lower edge of the Wrapped Knot.

Then cut the working cord (WC) to the correct length:
- The working cord (WC) would be ten yards long for 7 inches or less.
- The working string will be twelve yards long, for more than 7 inches.

16. Put set 1 on top of set 2. Hold the working cord (WC) right next to (or last) the 2 sets. Bring it to the bottom of the ring and then back to where you plan to continue wrapping.

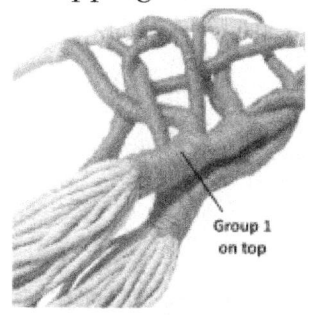

Start wrapping for at least an inch in brown area. When you hit the lower end of the GROUP 1 binding knot, put group three under the remaining 2, then cover 3 inches for another.

The reason to put the classes on top of one another other is to ensure your Tree Decoration is smoother from front to the back side, instead of being side by side. If you want a larger trunk this is unnecessary.

17. Divide the strings (core) from Cotton into two separate groups. Place only one party under the circle.

Choose a string from the center of the circle, and connect it using a Double Half Hitch (DHH) at the bottom of the chain. It will rest on the left side of your Half Hitches which you attached to the string used to seal the chain. A solo Half Hitch is seen on the graphic. Always sure that you fit in two.

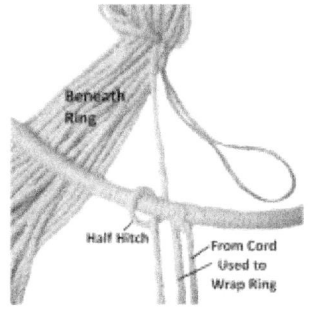

Put the remaining half of the string above the triangle. Take one cord from that set, and use a DHH to connect it to the chain. Place it on the right hand side of your knots made from the rope used to tie the ring.

18. Continue to tie the Wrapped Knot (WK), ensure that the 2 sets of Cotton cords remain at the same place. End wrapping until hitting ring bottom.

End the knot by going through the bent region at the working end. Push forward to hold the knot.

Hang the Tree Decoration at the top of the tiny circle, so you can focus on to your fringe. You may create a two layered fringe as mentioned below, or you can do the same length with the front and back cords.

These will represent the "roots" of your tree and you can create any length of them. The fringe was at 3 inches in the picture at the top of the list.

Find the cords behind the circle and cut them ten to fifteen inches below your ring. For strings in front of the ring the fringe would be shorter (6 to 8 inches long). Undo growing cord (usually 3 to 4 strands) absolutely.

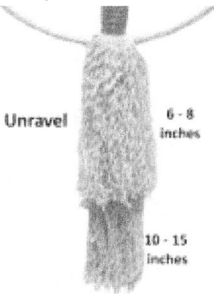

Unravel 6 - 8 inches 10 - 15 inches

19. You can wrap an artificial vine with leaves or artificial flowers to cover the brown cords so that it mergers in with Tree Decoration branches. Secure it on to the ring in many locations, and interlink it through a few branches.

Chapter 3: Macramé Patterns - Daily Use Items

The chapter provides detailed information of macramé patterns that can be used in our daily life to produce various products.

3.1 Hammock Chair

The Hammock Chair is quite simple to generate, yet it is time consuming because it is significant in size. It comprises of a net-like panel in one long piece, creating both the back and the bench. It bends upward to make deep pockets at the bottom edges.

This project in Macramé is ideal for beginners because of its simplicity. Before starting, you must ensure how to tie all the knots used in the design, especially if you are a beginner. The seat size is around 32 inches long. Increasing the size can be done by cutting extra cords. Ensure that the number of cords is a multiple by four.

Materials Required:

- Cord Length (size: 6 mm)
- Two 3-inch (heavy-duty) welded metal loop
- Elastic tape measure
- Cloth glue that dries completely

Knots used:

- Wrapped Knot
- Overhand Knot
- Barrel Knot
- Larks Head Knot
- Double Half Hitch (DHH)
- Alternating Square Knots (ASK)

Preparation (Cut the cords as follows):

- 16 strings, each of size 3.5 yards for upper side support

- 16 cords, each of size 4.5 yards for lower side support
- 32 strings, each of size 7 yards the seat
- Two strings, each of size 50 inches these would be for wrapping knots.

Step by Step Instructions:

1. Move 8 of the 4.5-yard cords into the ring then connect the ends. Tie the knots around the fence. Place on top of the previously bound cords 8 of the 3.5-yard cords, then fold and arrange them as well. Tie a knot wrapped around the strings, as laid out below:

2. Tie one side of a 50-inch chord to the right of the folded cords beside the bell. Move 2 inches down and continue winding this cord around the remainder of the cords. Restore the work-end to the area near the triangle.

3. Tie the working end around the strings, and also the locked end of the working string. Wrap firmly, then begin to push forward when near to the ground.

4. The folded part of Working Cord now looks like a shell. Across this loop move the working end of the working thread.

5. Pull the sealed portion, at the top binding point. This will push the end of the job by the Wrapped Knot, and the revolving circle formed by the working rope. Trim all of the cord flush's loose ends with both the top and bottom edges and drape the stubs inside where they are not noticeable. The resulting knot looks like the one on the pic.

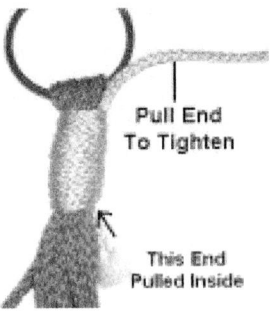

Pull End To Tighten

This End Pulled Inside

6. Recreate step 1, connecting the remaining 3.5-yard and 4.5-yard cords onto the other loop in the same manner. CAREFULLY take both rings on each string, and they keep the ring securely. They shouldn't trip on rings back and forth.

Connect the links to the desk floor, or put them up such that the cords are in an upright position. Choose 2 of the shorter strings from the right side ring (3.5 yard), and two more from the left side ring. The strings you choose will settle wherever they come off the Wrapped Knot. These cords are to act as supporting loops to the upper side of the Hammock Frame. Move down 36 inches from the bottom edge of the Wrapped Knot. The four cords are to be kept diagonally to each other, and they unite at this point. That would form the upper edge of your chair's back.

Mentally mark the left side cables as 1 and 2, and the right as 3 and 4. Crawl a simple Square knot using them. The active cables are 1 and 4, and the fillers are 2 and 3. To build the back and bottom of the Hammock Chair, you must connect the other strings on each side of this Knot. Hold the numbered ENDS to recall which cables to use in your next move. The result would be similar to the one in the photo below.

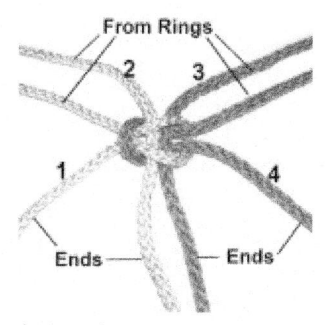

7. Move the ends of the four strings to the right and south, standing parallel to the section that descends from the rings. For all these four lines the back and seat cords of the Hammock Chair should be connected. Authors tip: This is best to operate on a flat floor, because it allows to conveniently place the lines, because the wires are horizontal. Curl one 7-yard

string in half and put it on top of the four holding strings on the Square knot's left. The fold is to be aimed at you. Take the halves under the holding cords and over the folded field and pull them to you. This knot is the Larks Head Knot (LHK) in reverse. Leave a tiny gap on the holding cord between the knot and the Square knot. Knots should be tightened

8. Tie the right half of the rope with a Half Hitch tie, by placing it to the right of the Larks Head tie. Pass it through the carrying strings, and then beneath. Place it around the operating cord when you bring it in next to you. Knot must be tighten. Now use the left half of the working cord to make a Half Hop on the Larks Head knot to the top. Tighten the knot in the same fashion as previously achieved. Move to the right of the initial operating thread, and it rests towards the Square Knot. Redo stage 5 with 7-yard cords left over. A minimum of 16 cables will be placed in the middle of the holding cords on either side of the SK. It is important that you calculate carefully at this stage, so that the ASK rows are matched correctly. Accurately calculate the number of sections, and the gaps are equivalent to the amount of side aids that you intend to deal with.

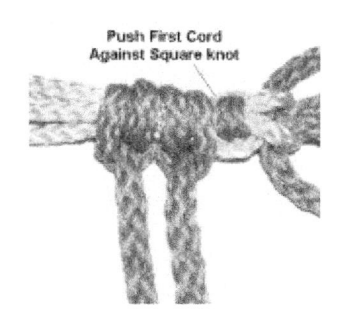

9. To make the Hammock Chair back side, tie 21 rows of Alternating Square Knots (ASK) to the 7-yard string. The starting row will contain the Step 5 mounting knots. The rest of the rows should be 1"apart. If you want the back to be shorter in size you can reduce this. In row 1, tie LEFT Square Knot with 1-32 cords, and RIGHT SK with 33-64 cords. Redo for the odd numbered rows left (such as 3, 5, 7, etc.).

In row 2, connect the LEFT Square Knot with 3-34 cords and RIGHT SK with 35-62 cords. Repeat the following even numbered rows cycle (4, 6, 8, etc.).

10. Then for the seat, strengthen the knots in row 22, so they lay 1/2 inch below those in row 21. Redo for remaining rows. If you like a tighter pattern, you should move the knots 1/4-inch apart, but make sure the panel is always stretched laterally. It is necessary to NOT tie the knots close together for the table. There must be at least some distance between rows or the panel is going to get too short. Stop when at least 23

rows have been joined (in this situation a minimum of 44 rows for both the back and the seat).

11. Hold the hammock chair with the support of the rings, if you haven't. Choose any two supporters from the LONG side (4.5-yard) that come from the right ring and two from the left ring. Diagonally transfer both of these cords into one another. It will be very much exactly what you did in step 3. From the Wrapped knot calculate at least 60 inches down. This is the location the cords are meant to touch. Tie the knot in the Square to briefly attach them. Place a seat on top of those carrying cords, to check the Hammock Chair's size. The seat has to move up, because it's at a small angle to the chair's back. But it does not rise up too high or the Chair of the Hammock would not be comfortable. Change the seat where the holding cords are tied; this will make the seat shift upwards or downwards. Keep practicing for the Square knot organization, before you prefer the seat size.

12. When the lower cords have entered a suitable location, tightly tie the Square Knot. Use fabric glue while tightening the knot. This should hold the knot securely sealed.

13. Instead of letting them hang, move the edges of the new holding cords so two go to the right and the other

two head to the left. Using Double Half Hitches to attach half the cords from seat to the right of the Square Knot, and the other half to the left. This is achieved exactly as in step 5; the only variation being the knot type used. Start in the center and move when you connect the cords (on both sides of SK) outwards. On the end of each cord tie a Barrel Knot, and it lies under the seat of the Hammock Chair, at the bottom edge. Finish the seat by choosing each of the two options: Trim the sides of the lines, but make sure that they are at least 2 inches long and move into the loops at the seat's BACK. Keep them in place using cement. Or you may cut the cords and leave a fringe, then mount them. At the bottom, attach a Barrel ties to avoid unraveling of the cords.

14. Arrange the cords left for helping the right hand into a pair of twos. You must start form the bottom and push up the top when you follow them to the back and sit on the right side. In row 42, the main side help is mounted right next to the SK, which at the end is two rows away from the double half brace. Slide one of the longer side (4.5-yard) supports through the space next to the Square knot. Do the same for the other string, bring it into another spot, next to the same SK. Make sure the supports at the side are vertical, with a little tension. Use an Overhand knot to tie the two strings together. Tighten the knots, and that meets the seat's

Edge. Attach an extra Overhand knot next to the first one. Making sure it stays at the back of the Hammock chair after securing this knot too. Pull the edges to the seat front before continuing to the next stage.

15. Redo step 11 with just the leftover LONG side supports, positioning them on the right side of the seat per 3rd section.

And do the same for the Small side helps, while you operate in the upper field where Square Knot's rows are farther apart. There will also be room in between the supports per three sides. Ensure sure you place the supports as similar as possible to the Square Knots, even though the spaces are more important.

16. It's helpful to bring the support cords down the entire right side in place, then go back and tie them with the knots. This way, if appropriate, you may make improvements to their place.

17. Follow measures 11 and 12 through installing supports on the left foot. If required, make the appropriate changes to the ties, so the Hammock Chair hangs equally, before going on to the next stage.

18. Go back to where you began and move into another space the ends of the new side supports like before, to the left. Now attach the cords again, using 2 Overhand Knots (OK), as performed in stage no 11.
Do this step for both sides on all sides on all other side supports current. Once finished, add the glue to the knots and allow it to dry before continuing.

19. To build a fringe using the remaining material from the side supports. OR you can use any extra ties to tie them to the table. Depending on your choice another alternative is to make Barrel knots at the end of both of the loose strings, so they rest near to the Square knots. Apply finishing glue then break off any excess content.
To tie the Hammock Chair to a thick branch or heavy-duty hooks in a ceiling post, using chain or rope to move them through the rings.

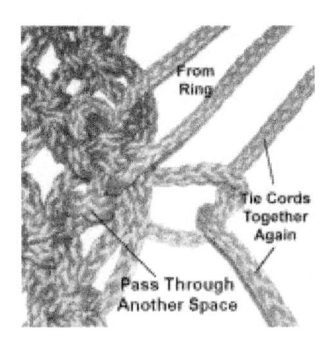

3.2 Macramé a Basket

This type of basket is attractive and fast to make. It's the best project for beginners who have some or no knotting skill and for those who are entirely new in this craft.

The size of the ring that you use to create the basket determines the size of the basket. It can vary from smaller to larger. This basket can hold everything you wish. It can be a little toy or an artificial plant or even a real fruit; the possibilities are endless.

Some basic Macramé knots are used to make this beautiful basket.

Knots used:

- Half Hitch (HH)
- Reverse Lark's Head (RLH)
- Half Knot (HK)
- Square Knot (SK)
- Half Knot Twist Sinnet (HK Twist)

- Wrap Knot
- Alternating Square Knots (ASK)

Materials Needed:

- 50 Yards of Macramé cord with a thickness of 5MM or 6MM. The strings should be Firm, not soft for such projects braided cords are ideal.
- One welded metal ring 6" round (It should not be a raw metal ring, must be treated, It is advised to use gold-tone)
- 1 Yard ribbon having the width of about 1". (Print or small design looks great for the contrast)
- Optional: One 6" Ceramic Sleeping monster
- Optional: A small plant. Use your favorite flower or plant as a floral accent to match or contrast with the cord.
- Knotting board (or plastic covered ceiling tile)
- T-pins
- Tape measure or yardstick

Step by Step Instructions:

1. Take 6" sized ring and bend it slightly to create an elliptical shape.
2. Cut 32 strings, one and half yards long and one string 1 yard long.

3. Find the middle of each string and independently Reverse Lark's Head (RLH) every string on the 6" ring. DO NOT RLH THE ONE YARD STRING. (Set the one yard string aside. This cord will help to tie the wrapping knot at its end.). Yeah, let's do an evaluation before we start binding the knots. Both cables will now be placed into the 6" ring except for the 1 yard cover cable. The ring will be lined with no display of metal. Do a Half Hitch (HH) for one of the connecting cords inside each class while metal is shown. Proceed with the directions in the next section, until ring is filled.

Some four strings in the ring are picked. Use the two main strings as functioning strings, and the two central strings as holding strings tie a 5 Half Knots (HK Sinnet) Sinnet. After entering the third HK they should begin to twist. Move to the next four strings. Plus 4 strings below. Do the Half Knot Sinnets binding groups all the way round the ring before both cords are knotted (in units of 4). Count cords when you move around the loop, and there are no strings remaining or tucked inside. Take care of the tightness too. Were you a loose knotter or a strong knitter? Whoever you are, be careful and bind all knots the same, so that rows can match themselves.

Now you are entirely near the ring and prepared to tie your first row of SK's.

Square Ties (SK's) Connect ONE row running all the way across the basket. Study the diagram so that you learn precisely what cords you can use. You won't need the same four commonly used cords to create the Sinnets Half Tie. Shift two cables on the side, and you'll use 2 cables from one Half Knot Sinnet and 2 cords from the other. Otherwise you'll add just more knots to the sinnets. Hope that will be practical for you. It is vital you tie the correct cords.

4. Fasten another series of SK's but this time will be the alternate row by joining Alternating Square Knots (ASK's).

5. Fasten three more rows of ASK's in the same manner. Once done, you will have to complete all the knots in the basket.

Your basket should now look like this.
1st row. One row of 5 Half Knots creating a twisting Sinnet.
2nd row. One row of Square Knots.
3rd row. One row of Alternating Square Knots.
4th row. One row of Alternating Square Knots.
5th row. One row of Alternating Square Knots.
6th row. One row of Alternating Square Knots.

6. Take all the strings and push them into the topmost ring (take inside out). Grasp all the strings and

Using 1 yard cord to tie a knot securely around all cords.

7. Turn the right side out. Make sure not to cut any of the cords because these cords will serve as a cushion for your tiny monster. Arrange all strings neatly in the basket. Look around the whole basket to make sure that no cords end are sticking to the basket openings.

8. Weave a ribbon in the remaining open spaces created by the HKS on the top of the basket. Tie a pretty bow or finish the ribbon according to what you like to create other than a bow.

9. Put your put inside basket or add a pillow or other toys if needed. (This step is optional).
Tuck in any floral twig to compliment your finished item. (Optionally)

10. You can make addition of a ring to the basket's bottom as well for a different appearance. If you use a bottom ring, you may require to Half Hitch all the strings to bottom of the ring before fastening the Wrapped Knot. The completed basket can be high or low. If you want the basket to rise bigger, raise it up on the top rim, or move it down softly if you like it lower.

11. Using any ceramic "laying or sleeping" creature 6 "long and 4" wide to ensure that it fits in a completed macramé basket deprived of reshaping the metal frame. Start placing ceramic toys inside the ring before beginning your project to ensure it fits inside the ring.

3.3 Designer Hat

This Macramé Hat has a round top and a beautifully decorated brim with tiny triangles. It can also be used as a Macramé basket. For this, it is recommended to use a material which is not extremely flexible, or it doesn't keep its shape. Bonnie Braid is used in the illustration given below.

A medium-sized hat with dimensions of 28 inches around with a 1.5-inch brim will be created here. If you want to make a smaller or larger hat, I have provided you with cord measurements.

It is a simple project for beginners. Be sure to practice the decorative knots stated under before you attempt to make this personalized hat if you're new to Macramé.

Materials Required:

- 4mm Cord Material (114 yards)

- Fabric Glue
- Tape Measure
- Pins and Project Board

Knots used:

- Alternating Square Knots (ASK)
- Larks Head Knot
- Overhand Knot
- Double Half Hitch (DHH)

Step by Step Instructions:

1. For the hat created here, you will need to cut 56 cords, which should be 2 yards in length each. For a 24-inch hat cut one holding cord 36 inches long and 48 other strings, each of which must be 2 yards in length. For a 32-inch hat, you will need a total of 64 cords, 2.5 yards each. For a hat above or below these sizes, increase or decrease the size as needed (2 strings per inch). The number of cords you use should be multiples of 4. Fix the split ends of the cord with a tape. It would prevent the unraveling of the strings. Tie the holding string with your work station horizontally, and make sure it is stretched firmly. Fold in half one of the two yard strings, and place it under the holding string, so that it lies near the center.

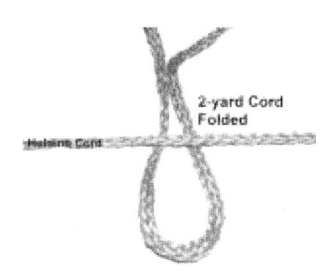

2. Place the ends over the holding cord to complete the formed Larks Head knot, going downward. Move them underneath the folded line. Stiffly close.

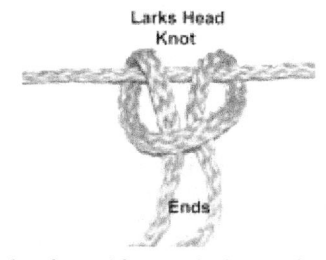

3. Attach each end of Half Hitch knot by leading the rope over and below the holding string. It will ride over the thread you're working with when you set it down.

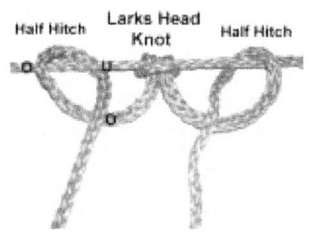

4. Repeat the steps from step 1 to 3, by wrapping the remaining strings to your holding string. Start working from the center and move to the ends.

There must be an equivalent amount of strings in both directions.

5. For creating the edge for your Macramé Hat, chose any eight cords and marked them from cord 1 to 8 from left towards right. All the triangle designs are created using eight strings, so split them out now, before you start working on the triangles. Make a Square Knot with 2-4 strings. You only have one filler the string 3. Tightly firm it, so it sets against your mounted knots. Do it again with the strings 5, 6, and 7. This time the filler is cord 6.

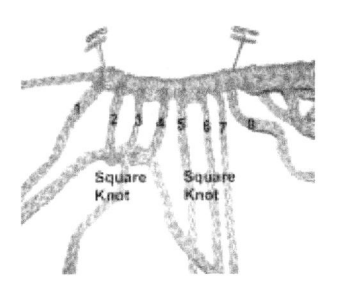

6. Now attach the other Square Knot under the first two, using strings 3 - 6 (two fillers -- 4 and 5). Tighten the knots firmly, so it rests over the knots above it.

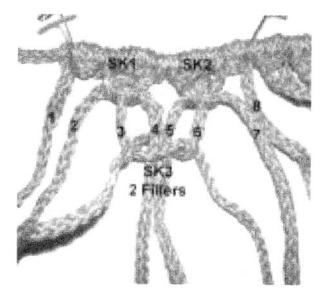

7. Move the cord number 1 with the left side of the three knots that forms a triangular shape. Lock it, so that it's tight since it is a holding string. Join the cords 2, 3, and 4 to it through the Double Half Hitches.

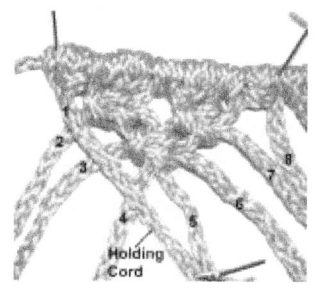

8. Move the string 8 along the right edge of the triangle, and fix it as well. Attach strings 5, 6, and 7 with it with a Double Half Hitch knot. Make sure not to attach the holding cord 1 with it, or the design will be unbalanced.

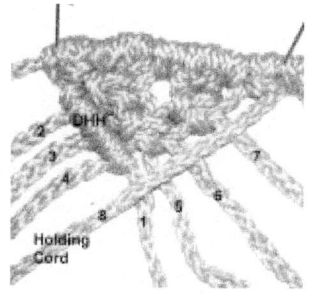

9. Make a cross using the firming string 1 and 8, and extent all the strings in a manner so it will be easier for you to see them. Attach a Square Knot using cords 1, 4, 5, and 8. Use cords 8 and 1 as the fillers. Firmly tie the knots, so that the knot stays below triangle level.

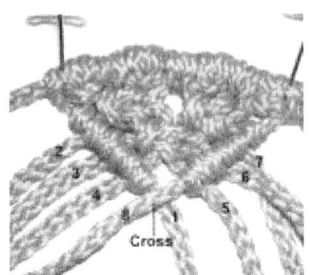

10. Repeat steps 5 to 9, to make additional triangle with the help of your next eight cords. Attach a Square Knot from the first line, with cords 6 and 7, and 2 and 3 from the second side. Tighten it so under each triangle it meets up with the Square Knot.

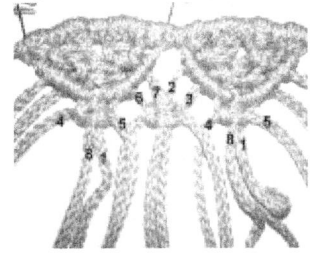

11. Repeat step from step no 5 to 10 with the help of remaining clusters of cords. When you reach the final triangle figure for your Macramé Hat, connect this triangle to the first triangle you created, to make a complete circle. Now begin turning upside down the brim of your Macramé Cap. Although actually the right side of the triangles is on the

opposite side of the hat. Keep in mind that the brim which is created will be folded in a manner, so the orders are swapped. It can be also be seen in the picture attached below, which is showing the rear side of the triangles at the moment, where you will be doing your work. Attach a Square Knot with the help of strings 2 and 3 from the first triangle that you created, with 6 and 7 from the last triangle. It is just what you have done in the previous step, and the only difference is that the cords come from each edge of the brim

Identify the edges of your holding string used in the tying process. Once you identify your holding cord, tie an Overhand knot and glue it, and tie another one on the upper side of the first knot. Trim the excess by 2 inches, fold them under the mounting knots, and apply a generous amount of glue so it holds the knots in its place. Don't forget that the triangles should be at the back side and not on the front.

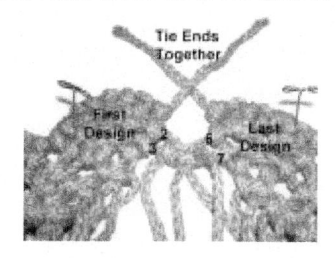

12. To create the top part, you will link a row of Alternating Square knots (ASK) using 4 cords per knot, two working cords, and two fillers. Starting at the place where the two ends were connected in phase 7 is easiest, then continuing around the entire route. To create the next row, alternate the strings. Keep the brim on the inner side while creating your hat. Mentally number each set with four cords. Strings No.1 and No.4 act as the working cords, while two and three are the filler cords. Combine 3 and 4 with 1 and 2 from next knot over to alternate for next lines. And the current knot lies between the two above.

13. Stop tying Alternating Square Knot when your Macramé hat is at least 7 inches in height which starts from the lower end of the brim, till the row of knots that you are currently working on. Keep in mind you'll cover the bottom, so you'll only have a couple more rows to add to the top.

14. Choose 12 cords that are coming from the three Alternating Square Knots. Visually mark each set with four cords as A, B, and C. Push all the four strings from the set B to the inside of the Macramé hat.

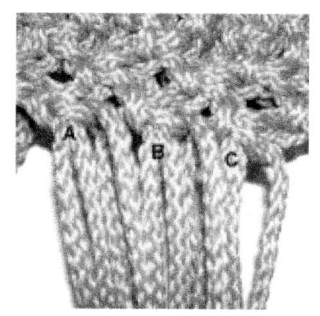

15. Use the cords 3 and 4 from set A (that is at the extreme left side), with strings No.1 and No.2 from your set C (that is at the extreme right side). With these four ropes, tie securely a Square Knot over the gap left by the strings you just put through. Tighten the knots firmly. So the top edge of your hat will appear more rounded.

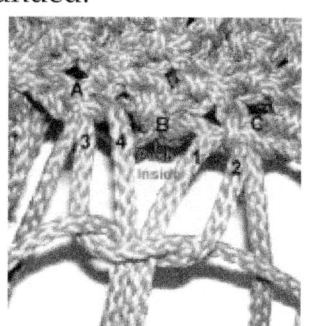

16. Repeat the previous step by dropping all the remaining knots by pushing the knots inside. This will fasten the top of the Macramé Hat. Do steps 3 and 4 two more times, until you've been all the way back. Move the remaining cords into the inside until you are done.

17. Take the right side of the hat up. Note, that the front of the triangles at the top is the bottom, and while you're focusing on these final stages, they can be

seen around the lower lip. Tie two very tight overhead knot using two cords at a time but from two different knots. If there are some wide gaps, begin crossing the void by choosing cords from each side of it. Hook one knot, apply adhesive to the thread, then tie the knot next to the previous. Trim the excess cords after you tie the knots. As the strings are taped at the ends, you can simply cut them off to identify which cords are used. After you are done with tying all the knots, let the glue dry and cut off any extra material. Switch the Designer Hat's brim outwards, arrange it at the triangular tip.

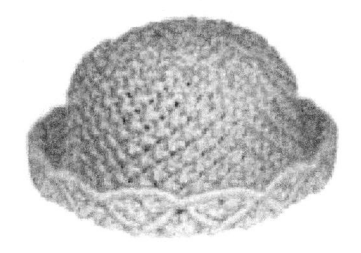

3.4 Macramé Pillow

Now we will learn how to create this beautiful DIY Macramé Pillow. It's not as complicated as it looks– the toughest part is to cut the long cords. After you create your design, detach it from your rod and re-join it to your pillow. It's really easy.

Knots used:

- Lark Head Knot
- Square Knot
- Double Half Hitch Knot

Materials Needed:

- Macramé Cord
- Sewing Machine/Thread (optional)
- Dowel or Stick
- Scissors
- Pillow cover and insert
- Tape Measure

Step by Step Instructions:

You can start with your pillow cover you have for this pillow, or create a simple pillow cover for any pillow available. Don't just make it yet-see first Stage no 5. In the illustration below, the pillow cover is made of drop fabric. This ended up exactly identical to the rope, which looks impressive.

However, if you do want to see the Macramé show, pick a different color for your pillow cover.

The cover in the picture is 20 x 20 inches, for reference. You have to ensure that your Macramé pattern can cover your pillow-but if not. The best news is if required, it can be stretched out.

1. The first step is the cutting of your cords. To make this pattern, you'll require 16-12-foot string. (And depending on how much you like the fringe, you'll have a little excess).
2. Using reverse lark's head knots tie all 16 cords to the dowel. You've learned how to tie a lark head knot to build the hat in the previous instructions.
3. For this cover, the pattern is the only rows of alternating square knots. Leave a little gap among each knot-around half of an inch as a reference. Having a little space makes the project run even quicker.

You have to keep making the alternating square knots till you get down to the 20 " edge. Measure using the tape to watch where you are.

Create two horizontal rows of (left-to-right, then right-to-left) double half-hitch knots until you touch down the bottom.

4. So, now that we're done with the design cut off the excess from the bottom but keep a piece of the fringe – about 5 inches or so. You may leave more or less, it's entirely up to you.

   So, you are either going to remove your pattern from the rod or just cut it off.

5. Break it off. Here's how you stick the Macramé design to your pillow. Before you stitch it up, whether you're making a cover by yourself – you're necessarily going to line up the design to the facade of the cover, leaving the cut edges a little over the top hang.

Place the back part over the cover, and Macramé design-right sides are facing each other-essentially you make a sandwich, and the Macramé design is called the "meat."

So, now patch your pillow cover's top edge-go above the cords too! Then it takes some degree of finesse, however you can fix it. Pin it all down to hold it all together.

Shove the Macramé pattern within your pillow to stitch rest of your pillow cover and stitch the remaining seams as usual.

Flip the right side up. Now you should have your Macramé pattern joined to the top of your pillow (comes out from inside between the seams).

Take another length of the Macramé cord and tie an easy knot on the back to attach the rest of the cover. Loop this string from out and in of square knots. Not only does this help spread out your pattern. Yet it must protect it down to the bottom too.

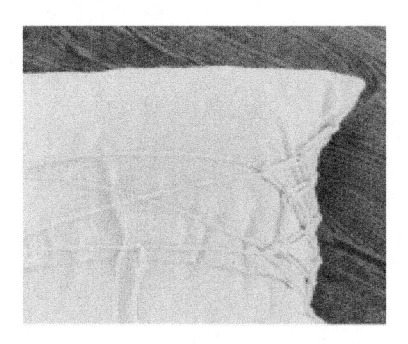

That is it! At the bottom edge of your pillow, the fringes will hang.

For A Ready Made Pillow Cover: You can open one of the joints and follow the instructions above or simply take the other piece of Macramé cord and thread it around the top. Then twist it backward. As mentioned above, you can also tie the sides.

Or, you could even hand stitch it to your pillow cover

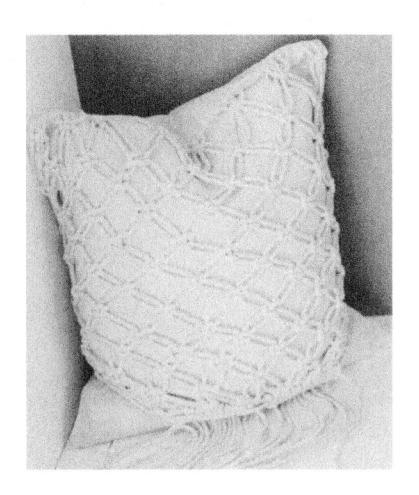

That certainly gives your sofa or easy chair a bit of an oomph. Yet this is sort of a novelty cushion – laying your head on it is kind of uncomfortable.

3.5 Window Belt

Window Belt has diamonds in the middle that are created with a traditional method. To create an oval-shaped opening in the middle of each of the diamonds, the strings are folded. The end is the braided knot.

This Macramé project is relatively moderate. You must need some practice for creating diamonds before you successfully creating this pattern.

Material Needed:

- 2mm String Material
- Project Board
- Tape
- pins

Knots used:

- Doubled Half Hitch
- Overhand Knot
- Interlaced Plaits
- Vintage Diamonds

Preparation:

For making the Window Belt, the first step is measuring the hips or waists. Cut twelve working cords, about four times the span you've just measured. Fix the edges with gum or an Overhand knot for all the cords. Cut two holding strings, each of which is at least one and a half times the span you are creating. Prepare these cables with the tape so that they can be clearly identified. Set all the working strings vertical, in two sets of six cords. The holding cord should be put among the two sets.

Define the middle by horizontally placing a section of tape over the region. You must start in the middle for the first interval of the Belt, and push near the one edge of the strings.

Step By Step Instruction:

1. For the Widow Belt, the first knot is connected only with the holding strings. Cross the cord left under the right one.

2. Using the left cord tie a Double Half Hitch in a clockwise direction to your right. So, the knot will be resting beside the tape.

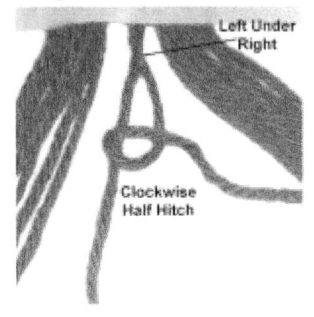

3. Organize the 2 holding strings on the top of working strings diagonally. The angle will be as similar as possible to a 45 degrees angle.

Useful tip: It is challenging to attach delicate strings so that they remain snug. So use one hand to lead the holding string when you tie the knots with the other. This will allow you to shift the holding cord if necessary in any direction.

In the illustrations below, the holding strings cannot be perfectly straight. They were tilted so that you could easily grasp the knots. Hold the holding strings straight and stiff all the time when doing this project.

In that order, connect working strings 6 to 1 to your holding cord. Ensure that each working string should be pulled straight before tightening each knot. The Half Hitches are now tied in the clockwise direction, as you move from left towards right.

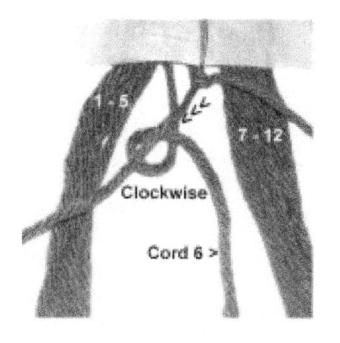

4. In that order, add cords 7 to 12 to your holding cord.

   The knots are connected in an anti-clockwise direction, as you move from left to right.

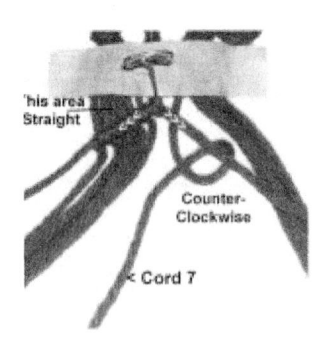

5. To begin the diamonds lower half, shift the left holding string diagonally to the right. Aim to create an angle as similar as possible to a 45 degrees angle. Organize and keep the working strings straight. Put a small pin at an edge, with holding cord on its outside.

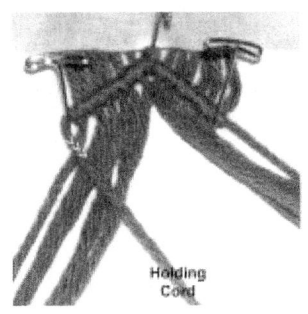

6. Locate your working string 6 that is nearest to the midpoint. Flip it over the other strings and heading left. Confirm that it lies under your holding string.

Tie the DHH in the counterclockwise direction, as you move from left towards right. Verify that it lies at a corner against the pin.

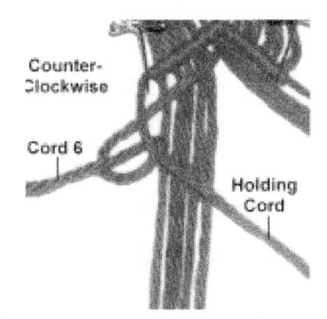

Attach cords 5-1 in the same way, each one folding above the others.

After adding a pin at the corner, move the right holding string diagonally to the left side. Attach strings 7 to 12 to the pin with DHH in a clockwise direction, each one folding over the other.

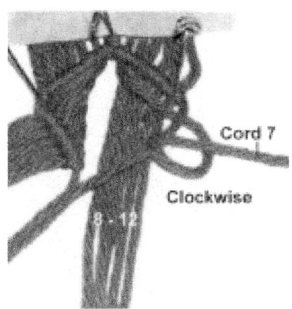

7. To finish a first diamond of the Window Belt, connect the left holding string with a DHH in a clockwise direction to your right holding cord. Drag your finger inside the diamond along the sides of a window to create it look as oval in shape as possible.

8. Repeat steps 2-6, becoming the first half of the permanent diamonds in the Window Belt. Make sure that you match sufficiently to allow 1/2 of the section that you're targeting for. For each diamond in top half, join cords 6 to 1 and 7 to 12 (in that order) with your holding cords.

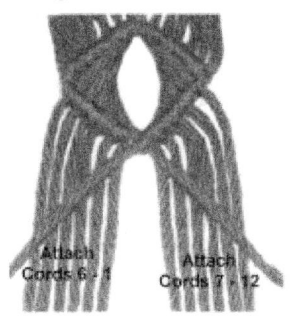

Aim to keep the cords straight in the field above the row on which you are working. Once all the pins are withdrawn, this will result in a gentle curve.

Start with cord 6 for the bottom half of each diamond, followed by cords 5-1, folding each over the holding cord at the left side.

Start with the string 7 on the right, then join cords from 8-12.

End the diamond through joining the left holding string to the right side.

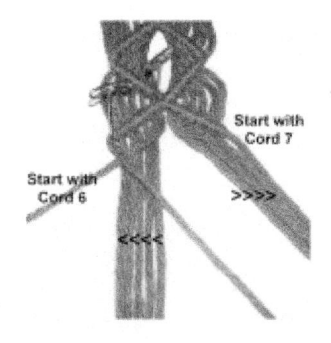

9. When the Window Belt's first half is completed, turn it around entirely and go back to the middle. To do the next half repeat from steps 3-7.

10. Fasten both of the ends of your holding strings by either using an Over-hand or a Barrel knot. When it's completed, apply glue and break off the extra when dry.

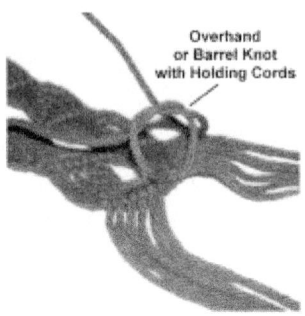

Now you'll make the braided which ties to shape the closure of your Window Belt. It is the optional step to follow, whether you like to make a particular type of clasp or closure.

11. Arrange the cords in three sets of four working cords and mentally tag them from left towards right. Switch group one to the middle between the two other groups. It must move over and above group 2.

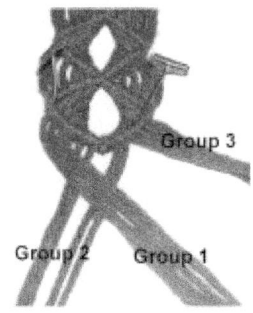

12. Now shift group three to the middle, among the two other groups. It will cross over group one.

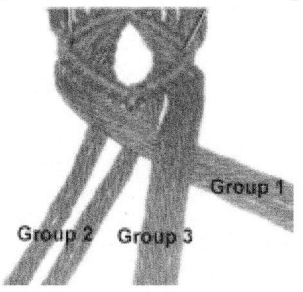

13. Moves group two to over group three. Now it's in the middle, between the two other groups.

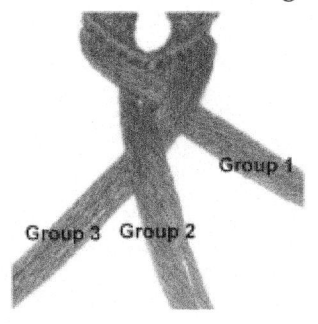

14. Repeat stage 10 to 12 to keep on weaving the tie. Pull as tight as possible, to get it secure at its place. Continue until it becomes 12-15 inches lengthy.

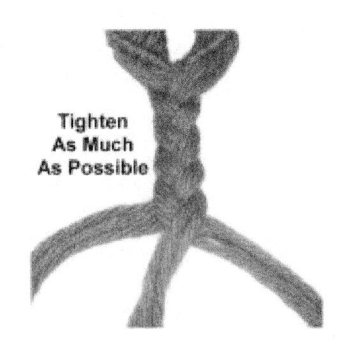

15. Use the whole group of strings to form the Overhand knot to protect the braid. Try to get the cords lined neatly. Cut the cords together to create a thin fringe.

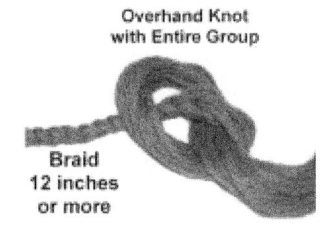

16. At the other end of the Window Belt replicate steps 10-14.

3.6 Shopping Bag

A Shopping Bag is generally similar to the net bags commonly seen in Europe. It is featuring wide-spaced rows of Alternating Square Knots that create a pattern on the fishnet.

The top ends are closely attached for some added support, and two loops are required for hanging and holding purposes.

This project is relatively serious as contrasted with other projects listed here. Beginners will not attempt this bag until they have already worked out any other designs. The finished height of the bag is around 18 "high. The area at the top is 9" wide. The bottom stretches to 15 cm, when extended laterally. When made from 24 ply cotton string fiber it can handle over 15 pounds.

Useful Tip: The Macramé Bag is constructed in two (front and back) parts.

- Start by taking steps 1-5 to create the first brace. The first knot is connected in the center of the ties, and you operate on both ends.
- At stage 6, you do a second strap.
- You then start the front piece at steps 7-21 by attaching the operational strings to one string.
- You then repeat the loop to create the back piece in step 22.
- You fasten all halves to the sides in step 23.

You make the remainder of the bag in steps 24-30 and finish off the bottom, going all the way through the two halves of the Shopping Bag.

Materials Required:

- 4 mm cord material (125 yards)
- Fabric glue that dries clear
- Measuring tape
- Project Board and pins
- Rubber bands

Knots Used in Design:

- Alternating Square Knots

- Larks Head Knot
- Square Knot (Left and Right)

- Overhand knot

Step by Step Instructions:

1. You'll start by creating one of the Shopping Bag belts. Cut 4 strings, each roughly 4.5 yards lengthy. And two more loops, lengthwise around 3.5 yards. Make the tips to avoid chain break (tape fits fine).
   Organize the cords upright and bind to the CENTER. They ought to be in the following positions: The 4.5-yard strings should be in 1, 3, 4, and 6 places. The 3.5 yard long cords are at 2 and 5 positions.
   You must make Square ties both right and left for the belts. The instructions below are for LEFT SK which is made with 1-4 cords. If you

touch left SK in certain sections of the Shopping Bag, the same general instructions can be used.

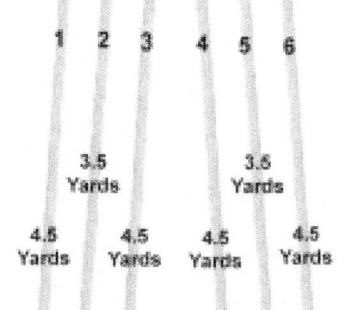

```
 1   2  3   4  5   6

       3.5        3.5
      Yards      Yards
  4.5      4.5   4.5      4.5
 Yards    Yards Yards    Yards
```

2. Both the strings in the strap are internally labeled 1-6. Running strings is 1 and 4, while 2-3 was filler lines. When the first knot is bind, remove the 5-6 chain to aside. Shift the cord no 1 over the filler cords and pass from left to right below the operating chord 4. Move the cord no 4 under the cords of the filler, then go back to left over cord 1 Pull the working cords 1 and 4 to secure the first half of the Left Square Knot. Let it lie back on the film.

Useful tip: The rule to remember when making Square Knots in opposing directions is that the head of the knot needs to face the orientation of the first operating rope you are going. So an LEFT Square Knot starts by moving the chord to the left which is chord 1.

After completion of these four measures, the head needs to turn left. So the 1 and 4 operating cords must have swapped positions in there. Shift cord no 1 above the filler cords and switch from right to left under cord no 4. Shift cord no 4 under the fillers, then move left to right over cord no 1. Pull-on cords 1 and 4 to extend the Square Knot to the second part. Then you have to find various cords

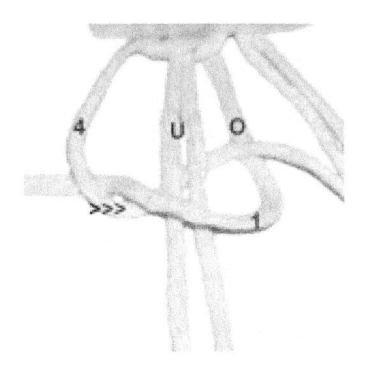

3. To build the zigzag design for the strap, you need to tie the knot backwards. The directions for your RIGHT SK are mentioned below. You should follow the same simple instructions as you're focused on certain parts of the Shopping Bag. The working strings used are 3 and 6. Strings 4 and 5 are fillers. Push the cord no six over the 4 and 5 filler cords and go under cord 3, right to center. Your functioning cord 3 moves through the fillers and over cord 6, going from left to right. Taut the first half of the Right Square Knot until it is past the corresponding knot. Sure it's not tipped. Now the 3 and 6 operating cables have to have places swapped.

Shift cord 6 over the fillers, then switch from left to right under cord 3. Underneath the filler strings, transfer cord 3 over cord 6 and switch right to center. Tie the tie.

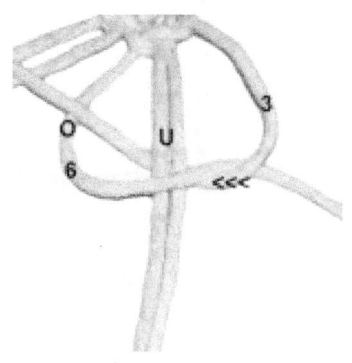

4. Continue to generate this zigzag pattern by forming a left Square Knot (SK) with cords 1-4 accompanied by right Square Knot (RK) using cords 3-6. Continue creating this alternating design until at least 7 inches of duration is in the first half of the band. Using Cords 1 and 6 to form one more Square Knot (SK). There will be four 2-5 filler strings. This will face the opposite way from the last bonded knot, since the same pattern continues.

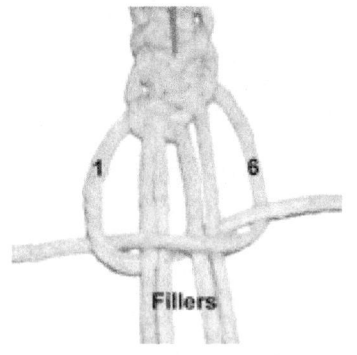

5. Rotate the strap around on the work surface until it's done, and switch to the center. Renumber all cords in the visual context. Repeat the 2 -4 steps to create the second half of that same strap. The first knot you make will be a left-wing SK.

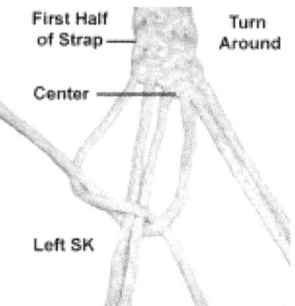

6. To make an extra strap implement steps 1-5. Place the new strap in front of the first strap as you start step 5, and compare its lengths. Begin to attach the second strap it becomes equal in length to the first strap.

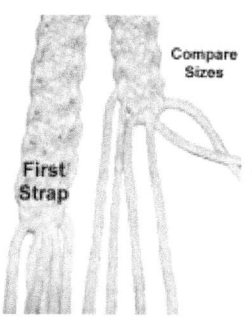

7. Then it's time to attach the Shopping Bag working strings that are attached to the straps. You'll only use one string at a time, so put aside the other rope for now. Straps must be fold, and the cords face up to you. Mentally mention the six fibers that arise in the left half of the strap. Mark the 1 and 6 strings, so you can easily identify them. Use the same with the strings that come from half the strap correct. Locate string 6 coming from the bag holder's left leg, and then move it sideways to the center. Pinpoint strand 1 from the right side of the strap, shifting it horizontally to the left side. Ensure they build a certain stress in the strings.

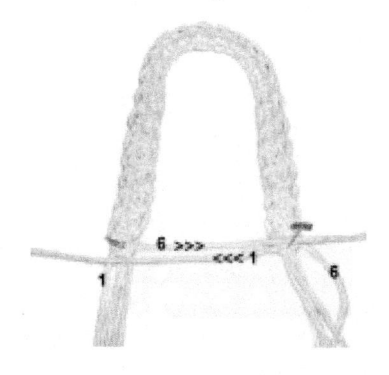

8. The bag's functioning cords will be linked to the holding cords that operate together. Think of them as if they were one big cord.

   Useful tip: Do not attach the operating cords to the cords you carry. Yeah, it's not going to create a loop.

   If you have performed the following steps, between the two halves of your strap, there should be a simple series of Larks Head knots. It should turn up as the one in the photo below. Cut six working strings, each 2.5 yards long. Prepare the edges to avoid unraveling. Divide one functioning string in half and put it underneath both of your holding strings in the middle of the pattern.

   The middle fold will move forward. Build a Larks Head Knot by drawing the two halves of the working cord towards you, passing over the holding strings, and into the folded area of the working cord. Squeeze the operating cord to secure the knot firmly.

Larks Head Knot

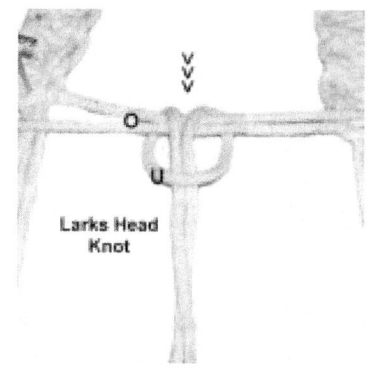

9. Using the left half of the working cord, create another Larks Head knot, follow the two-step method mentioned below: pull the left half over and under the holding strings, turning it in a clockwise direction. Bring it towards you. To complete the loop, pass it over itself. Firmly tie the knot until the loop sits on the left-hand side of your first Larks Head knot (LHK).

   Create a second ring to the left side of the first, by moving down the left half of your working cord under and over the holding cord, turning it in a clockwise direction. To complete the loop, roll it under itself and pull it up towards you. Firmly tighten the knot.

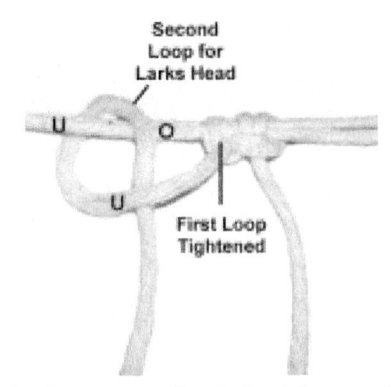

10. Slide the knots to the left side, so that the second knot sits against the strap.

Repeat step 9 using the cords to the correct part. This is generated by spinning the two loops in an anti-clockwise direction. The second loop is generated on the first to the right.

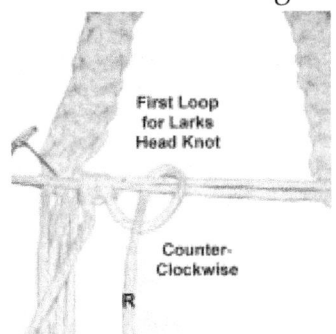

11. Repeat the 8-10 steps by attaching the remaining 5 of your functioning cords to the same band on your holding cords. Push on the holding cords until all of the cords are attached, so the ties align closely with each other, as shown in the image below. Arrange the knots as needed so this Shopping Bag's upper edge is clear.

12. Now shift the four cords that you were holding to another side. These are marked at the bottom and finding them will be simple for you.

    The remaining strings are the functioning cords (4 in number) from each half of your harness, along with the ones you just tied.

    A minimum of 20 cords are to be located in your row 1.

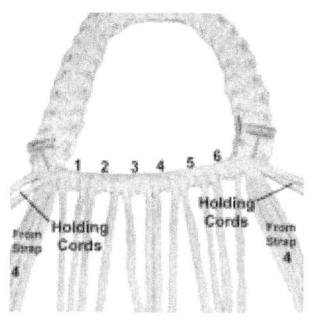

13. Now connect the first row of Square Knots with the below strings: Left Square Knot: using cords 1 − 4, 5 − 8 and 9 − 12 Right Square Knot: using cords 13 − 16 and 17 − 20 Tightly secure the ties so they remain near to the Larks Head Ties..

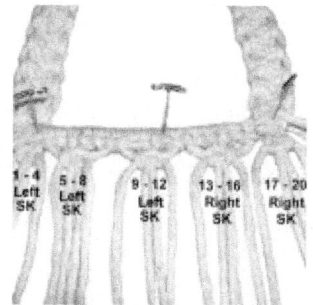

a. Repeat stage 16, adding a further 2.5 yard string to all sides of the diagonal holding cords. Rationally number the all the cords from 1 - 28, and attach the 3rd row of Alternating Square Knot using following strings:

Left Square Knots: Cords used are 1 - 4, 5 - 8, 9 - 12, and 13 - 16

Right Square Knot: Cords used are 17 - 20, 21 - 24, and 25 – 28. Now keep on adding more working strings in the same way. All that changes here are the lengths of the strings: Cut four strands, each of which is 2-yards long. Fix the tips to stop the ends from unraveling.

b. Fasten a two yard string to your diagonal holding strings on either side of your bag by help of the same method as defined in step no 16. Rationally number the all the cords from 1 - 32, and fix the 4th row of alternating square knots using the strings mentioned below:

Left Square Knot: Cords used are 1 - 4, 5 - 8, 9 - 12, 13 - 16

Right Square Knot: Cords used are 17 - 20, 21 - 24, 25 - 28, and 29 – 32

c. Repeat step 19 by attaching one of the 2-yard string to the diagonal holding strings on either side of your bag. Rationally re-number all the cords from 1 - 36. Tie the 5th row of ASK:

Left SK: Cords used are 1 - 4, 5 - 8, 9 - 12, 13 - 16, and 17 - 20

Right SK: Cords used are 21 - 24, 25 - 28, 29 - 32, and 33 – 36

d. Repeat the step 19, by attaching another 2-yard cord to the diagonal holding cords on either side of the bag. Mentally re-number all your cords from 1 - 40. Tie the 6th row Of ASK:

Left Square Knot: Cords 1 - 4, 5 - 8, 9 - 12, 13 - 16, and 17 - 20

Right Square Knot: Cords 21 - 24, 25 - 28, 29 - 32, 33 - 36, 37 – 40

e. Fold the other strap pattern that you set aside earlier and will be used to create the Shopping Bag's back portion. Repeat all the steps from 7 to 11, by mounting the 6 of the working cords to No.6 strap.

Redo all the steps from 12 to 21, by adding new strings to create the upper region.

f. Now Place the Shopping Bag front piece to your left, and the back piece to your right. The 6th row of knots will match up on every part. Those diagonal rows on which you have inserted the cords will create a design of V. Tie a SK with the 4th designated holding cords that connect the two parts together. To join the other side, you need to put the front side on top of the backside. Make sure that the inner sides are touching together, and the straps are not twisting. Tie the remaining four cords labeled, with a Square Knot. In the same manner.

Front on top of Back

B
F

SK With Holding Cords

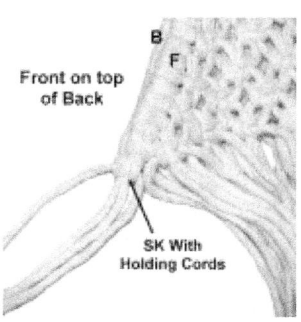

g. The left over rows of Alternating SK are tied around all parts of the Shopping Bag all the way back. Start from the one side, where the front and back are connected. Shift knots orientation (LSK or RSK) so they suit those in the above lines. In the picture below 7th row of your ASK can be seen. That was tied to both the halves of the bag. In this section, the ties will lay 1-inch below those in row 6. The other rows in step 25 will be no more than 1.5 inches away from each other. Do not lift the difference; otherwise the bag will spread too far.

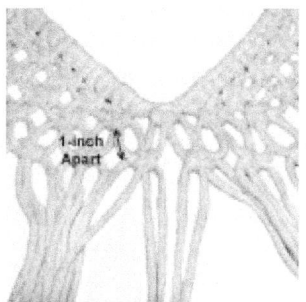

1-inch Apart

h. Keep on tying more rows of ASK till the Macramé bag reaches 18 inches in length from the top tip down to where you are presently working. Also you can increase the length if you are having sufficient material (more than 8 inches).

i. When you are at the last row of your Alternating Square Knots (ASK), taut them, thus they sit just below your previous row. No space should be left between them. It will help to strengthen and stabilize the bottom of the Macramé Bag.

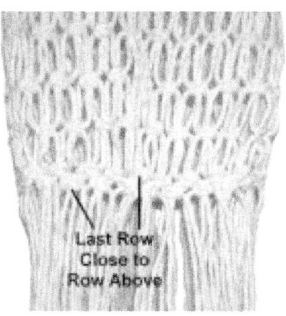

Last Row Close to Row Above

j. Take the bag inside out, now the knots will be on inside. Set the bag on the project board with the front on top of the backrest. Start from the left side; identify the first Square knot at both the front and the back parts. Bring all the ties together and lock them with a pin. In the next step, you'll just need those 8 cords.

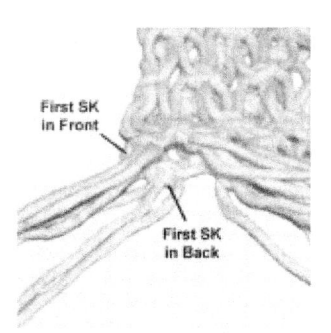

Arrange the strings, and there are a total of four sets of two strings each, combining one from the rear with one from the center.

Attach an Overhand Knot (OK) to a pair of strings. Then add the gum, and then attach a second knot overhead. Perform this process for the remainder of the three chord pairs, and cut the left over wires down to 1-inch.

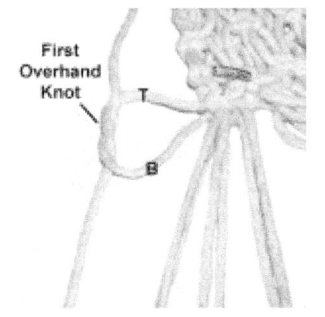

k. Once all the cords from knot 1 are tied off, match knot 2 from the back and front as well. Repeat step no 28.

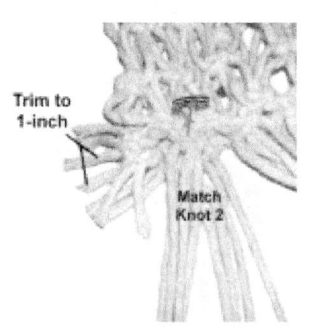

1. Repeat step 28 with all the strings that are left.

It's necessary to take time and match all the knots before you tie them since it's easy to lose your place. Focus on few strings at one time, to assure that all of the strings are tight, and the bottom is completely closed.

Chapter 4: Macramé Patterns-Latest Decoration Ideas

The chapter gives detailed information about Macramé Patterns to make latest decoration designs. With the help of these patterns you can make high quality stuff like the one available in market

4.1 Macramé Rose

This Macramé Rose is very easy to create, which is also a beautiful decoration. Although it is a time-taking project, but the final product is worth the investment. The petals formed using Double Half Hitches (DHH) set in longitudinal groups that bend at the more economical end. The resulted flower will have a sum of seventeen petals in 4 different sizes.
It is advised to use acrylic Yarn to make this Macramé flower. This way, the frond will be more comfortably shaped, and the tie created will be tiny and also easily adjusted. You need to use a material that can be blended easily during the ending phase, so nylon item or acrylic yarn works best for this kind of project. If using satin, keep in mind that the adhesive will permanently smudges the article, and the ties won't be strong enough.
Ensure before using the material, you test it by put on a flame to it, just to ensure it melts down and does not burn. And, check the glue on a small portion of the

material to confirm it will not permanently blacken the product as well and dries transparent.

This project is simple and fit for newcomers. The most difficult element is managing the delicate strings used in this creation. Ensure you know how to distinguish between holding cords and working cords.

Knots used:

- Double Half Hitch (DHH)
- Reverse Larks Head knot (RLHK)
- Overhand knot (OK)
- Wrapped Knot (WK)

Materials Needed:

- 2mm of any SYNTHETIC material such as polyester, yarn, nylon, etc. sixty two yards
- Glue for fabrics or any Household glue
- A Project board
- Pins, Tape
- Lighter or matchstick

Step by Step Instructions:

1. First of all, you will make the tiniest petals that will be the bud in the center of the Macramé Rose. For this, you will need two holding cords of lengths 9 inch and 20 inch and five working cords (WC) each

of size nine inches. To prepare these strings, create an Overhand knot (OK) at both edges of your holding cords (HC), so you can easily identify them. Fasten tape to the edges of your working cords (WC) so they are recognizable as well. All of the holding cords (HC) for the Rose are fixed with Reverse Larks Head knot (RLHK), as illustrated.

2. Order the cord that is 20-inch in length, hold it horizontally to your work surface. Ensure it has some pressure. Mentally mark it as holding cord marked A. Fold the other of your holding cord (HC) in half and mark it as Cord B now put it on top of your holding cord marked A, including the ends directing towards the rear end of your board. Take the edges of your holding cord B underneath cord marked A, now pull them towards yourself. They will pass over your previously folded section of cord B. Join the ends and pull on to the cords tightly so the knot you created tightens.

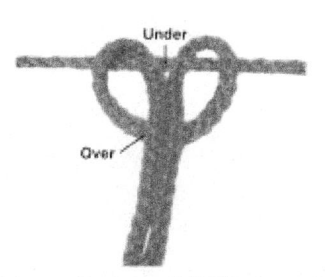

3. All of the Working Cords (WC) for the Macramé Rose is joined to two holding cords (HC) with the help of a Double Half Hitches knot (DHH). Every

time you start making a new petal, no matter the size, you will join the working cords (WC) to the holding cords (HC) in the center of the cluster. In this situation, you will join them to the two halves of holding cord marked B. Theoretically, marked them one and two. Now connect holding cord 1 (left) vertically, extend it, so it has some stress. Push a working string under both of your holding cords (HC). The middle should hold between them. Now keeping the working cord (WC) in the middle while you retaining the right part of this to your work surface. Put a pin near the holding cord (HC) marked two.

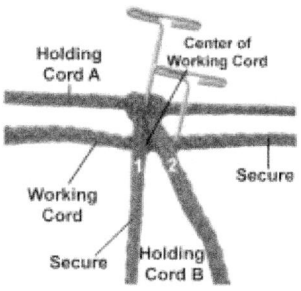

4. Tie a Half Hitch in anticlockwise direction with the left part of the working cord (WC) on the holding cord. A Half Hitch knot is made by creating a loop, over or under your holding cord (HC). As you pull it to your left hand side, pass over to create the circle.

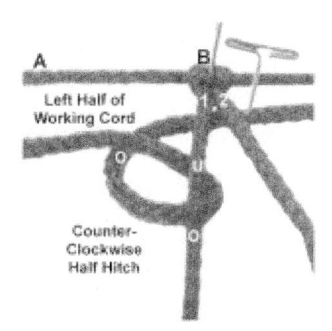

5. Bind the knot securely, and then tie the other knot onto holding cord (HC) 1, to create a Double Half Hitch (DHH).

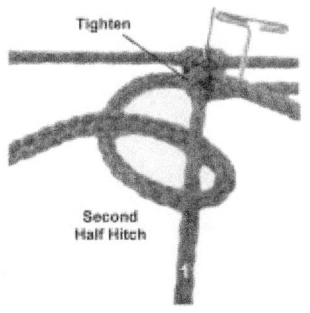

6. Simply remove the pin that you were using to hold the petal. Now use the right side of the working cord (WC) to make a clockwise Half Hitch knot (HHK) onto the holding cord marked 2. But don't tighten it just yet.

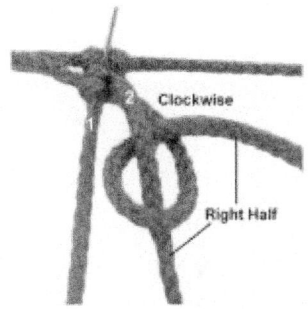

7. Pull on to holding cord (HC) no 2 towards your first Double Half Hitch (DHH). In this situation, that is to your left side. Tighten the newly created Half Hitch knot entirely. The goal of moving your holding cord (HC) to your other knot is to help slim the hole between them. Your Macramé Rose looks much neater if DHH's rows are close to one another.
8. If you tightly tie all the knots as much as physically possible, the rows would appear a lot neater. Every time you tie up a new Double Half Hitch (DHH), you can repeat this process. Now tie a second half Hitch knot (HHK), pull on to the holding string to your left while tightening again. Do straighten the holding chord after both Half Hitches (HH) are attached. This will cause the tie to rest next to the other tie in a proper position

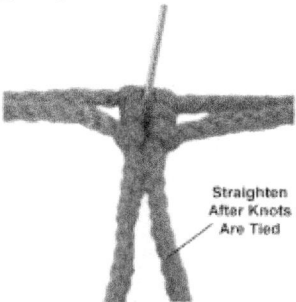

Straighten After Knots Are Tied

9. Repeat the steps from step no 3 till step no 7 to join the remaining of your working cords to your holding cords 1 and 2 there will be a total of five

strings to join. Don't let the knots to overlap, or they won't look neat.

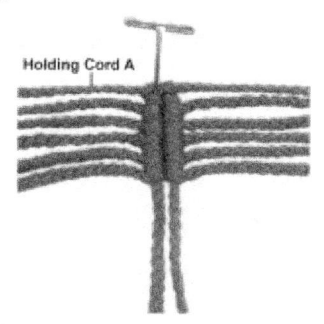

10. Move your holding cord (HC) no 1 underneath cord no 2, and then join it with a single Half Hitch (HH) knot in a clockwise direction. As you are creating the remaining petals for the Macramé Rose, you will join each pair of rows in this fashion.

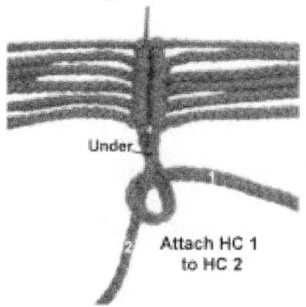

11. For finishing the Macramé Rose use glue to attach the working cords (WC) onto your holding cord marked A, that creates the outer end of every petal. Add a drop of glue on to your holding cord (HC) before you tighten the Half Hitches (HH) knot with each of your working cords. Some glue may leak out, so be sure to check it on working material before using it to ensure that the glue dries transparent and does not stain the

material permanent. Take both pieces of your holding cord marked A now add each and every one of your working cord to them, along with your holding cords numbered 1 and 2. Tie a Double Half Hitch at the left in a counter-clockwise direction and a clockwise Double Half Hitch at the right side. Ensure you stretch your holding cords toward the preceding rows while tightening each and every knot.

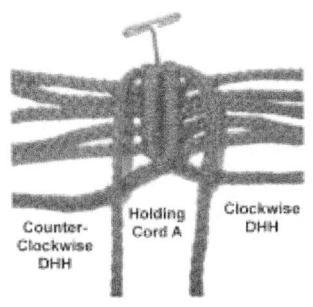

12. Slowly pull on both the halves of your holding cord marked as A, until the tip of the petal appears curved. Move the left side of holding cord A under the right side, and knot a Double Half Hitch (DHH) in a clockwise direction.

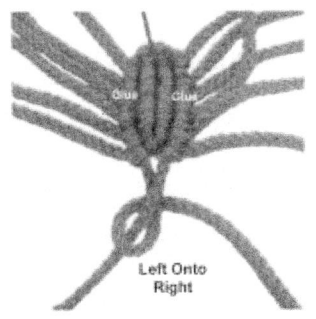

13. Redo the steps from step 1 till 11 a total of 2 times more to make 3 tiny petals of the same size.

14. For your Macramé Rose, you'll now create meddle-sized petals. You'll have a total of 3 holding cords (HC), two vertical and one at the very top. This will make the petals broader and lengthier than the tiny ones you just created. For this, you are going to need three holding cords two of length 12 inches and one of size 20 inches and five working cords (WC) each of size 11 inches. Ready the tips just like you did with the tiny petals. Organize the holding cord marked A that is 20-inch in size flat on your work surface. Use a reverse Larks Head knots to fix the other two of your holding cords (HC) onto it as you did in phase 2. Mentally mark the four cords from 1-4.

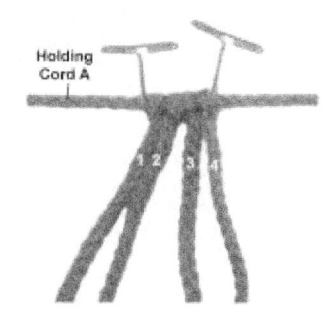

15. Repeat the steps from step no 3 till 8, by joining the 5 working cords (WC) to your holding cords (HC) no 2 and 3. Move the holding cord numbered 2 underneath cord 3, then join it with a solo Half Hitch (HH) knot.

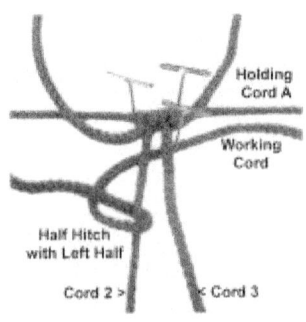

16. Pull down holding cords (HC) marked 1 and 4, and join the working cords (WC) to them with the help of Double Half Hitch knot. Attach the holding cords marked 2 and 3 to them as well. Keep in mind to pull all the holding cords (HC) towards the former rows of Double Half Hitch, as you are tightening every knot. To join the two lines of knots to one another, pass the holding cord numbered 1 under cord numbered 2, then tie a solo Half Hitch Knot (HH).

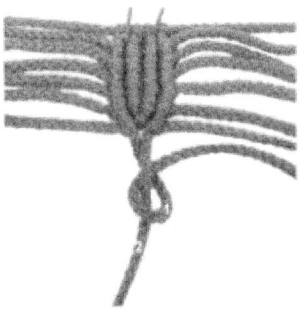

17. Fetch down both shares of your holding cord marked A, and connect the other strings with the help of DHH knot to them. Before tightening the Half Hitches (HH), ensure you apply some glue to it. To finish the Macramé Roses medium petals, slowly tug on both splits of your holding cord

marked A to allow the edge to be more rounded. If the petal curves from the mid, it's Fine, since it should be bent rather than smooth. Tie a Double Half Hitch knot in a clockwise direction while moving the left side of your holding cord below right.

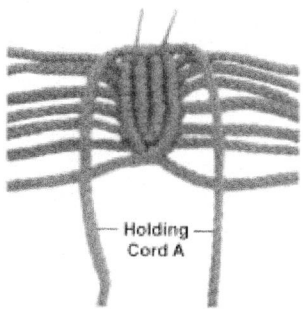

Holding Cord A

18. Repeat the steps from step 13 till 16 at least 3 more times, to make overall 4 more petals.

19. Now you are going to make the larger petals for creating your Macramé Rose. The only exception is you have three vertical holding cords to hold together with holding cord marked A to the top. Your holding cord marked A is shaped differently in order to facilitate the end to bend at the tip. For this, you will need four holding cords three of length 14 inches while one of length 20 inches and five working cords (WC), each of which has length 13 inches. Ready the strings in the same manner as you did with tiny petals. Secure the holding cord marked A of size 20 inches into an upturned V figure. Add one holding string with the help of

reverse Larks Head (RLH) knot to it, at the top in the center point.

Wrap the remaining two of your holding cords on both side of the first string. Assure the Larks Head knots (LHK) bends at the edge. Number the holding cords (HC) mentally from 1-6.

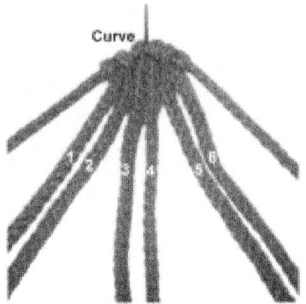

20. Repeat the steps from step 3 till 8, by attaching five of the working cords (WC) to your holding cords (HC) numbered 3 and 4. Once you are done, move the holding cord numbered 3 under the 4th, then tie a solo Half Hitch (HH) knot.

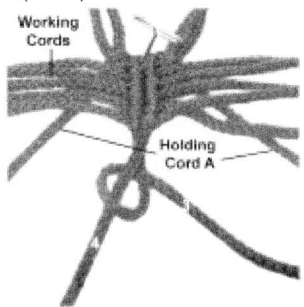

21. Bring down your holding cords numbered 2 and 5. Now join the working cords as well as the holding cords numbered 3 and 4 to it. Connect all the rows by moving holding cord (HC) 2 under 5, and then tie a solo Half Hitch (HH).

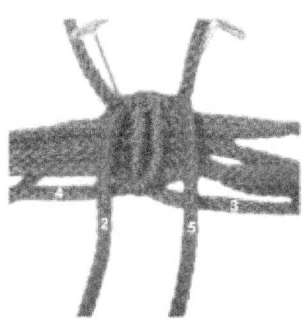

22. Transfer the two ends of holding cord (HC) A near one another, so that they are vertical to each other. This will aid the top end of the petal to become more curved. Bring down the holding cords (HC) one and six. And join the working cords (WC) as well as the holding cords (HC) that you were holding previously.
Now transfer holding cord one under cord six, and tie a solo Half Hitch (HH) to join the rows.

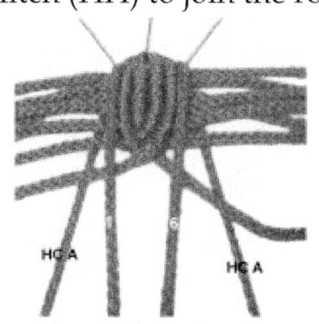

23. Take down both the halves of the holding cord (HC) A. Tie the other strings to this cord by using a DHH knot. Apply the glue at the end of each knot. Pull tightly on both splits of holding cord (HC) A to complete the wide petal for the Macramé rose to make the central region angled instead of being smooth, and to make the end more round. Now

transfer the left part of this holding cord (HC) under the right side, then tie a clockwise Double Half Hitch (DHH) to connect them.

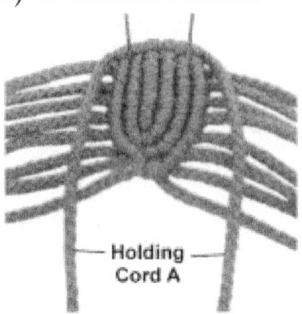

Holding Cord A

24. Repeat the steps from 18 till 23 at least 4 times to make a sum of 5 big petals in the same manner.
25. The outermost petals for your Macramé Rose are a little bit bigger than ones you created before. It's very essential that these be as curved as probable, mainly along the upper ends. For this, you will need five holding cords, four of which have length 18 inches and 1 with length 20 inches and five working cords (WC), each of which has length 16 inches.
26. Arrange the holding cord marked A of length 20-inch horizontally, then wrap the other remaining four holding cords (HC) to it with the help of a reverse Larks Head (RLH) knots. Curve the knots to create a curvy reversed V figure. Tight them well, so they can't uncurl. Mentally marked the eight holding cords (HC).

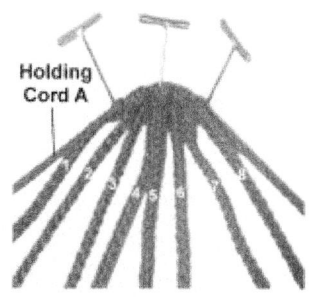

27. Repeat the steps from 3 till 8, by joining the five working cords (WC) to your holding cords (HC) four and five. Pass the holding cord (HC) 4 under 5, and join them by tying a solo Half Hitch (HH).

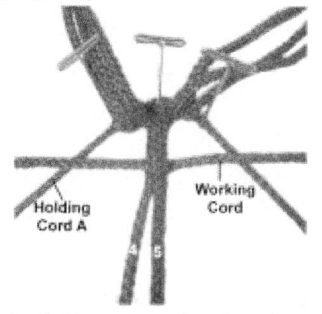

28. Take down the holding cords (HC) in couples, in the order as following 3 and 6, 2 and 7, 1 and 8. Attach all the working cords (WC) to them, with any other holding cords that you previously used. Keep in mind to connect the 2 rows at the lower end by tying a solo Half Hitch (HH).

29. Now bring down both halves of holding cord (HC) A, then join all the remaining cords to them with the help of a Double Half Hitch Knot. Keep in mind to add a small portion of glue to secure the knots. Pull-on the holding cord (HC) A, so that the petal

forms a curve and is neatly curved at the upper end. Now pass the left-hand side under the right, and tie a Double Half Hitch.

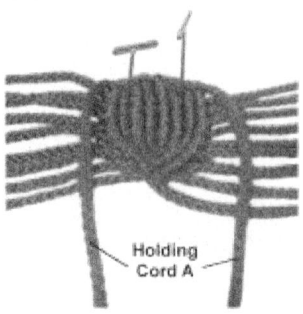

Holding Cord A

30. Repeat the steps from 25 till 28 at least 4 more times, to create a total of 5 outer petals.
31. For finishing the Macramé Rose petals cut off certain strings, and melt the stubs to make the edges neat and clean. The working cords (WC) were taped at the ends so that they would be easily identifiable. But for the holding cords, you will need to total them to define which holding cords to keep whole.

32. For the three minor petals, cut off all the working cords (WC) that is near to the outer ends. Be extremely precise. Make sure you don't cut off any knots.
    Now use the BBQ lighter to soften the tiny stubs. After adding the flame, immediately press the edges beside the table or any hard surface. This will help the molten part of the stubs to flatten, so the ends look neater.

33. Identify your Holding cord (HC) A, which has the tie on its ends. Separate them as they won't be needed in this phase. The other 2 of the holding cords (HC) are used to join the petals with one another. Place 2 petals beside each other. Now pass the holding cord (HC) from the left side petal under the right side, and make a Double Half Hitch knot. Add glue before tightening the knot.

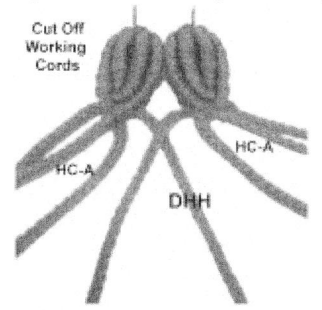

34. Repeat the previous step, to connect the 3rd petal to the second one. And then the first one in the similar fashion.

    Position the 3 connected petals, so they are joining each other, and use adhesive at the ends to make sure they hold their place. Now wrap some adhesive tape around them make sure the glue dries first. When the adhesive dries cut off the strings that were used to connect the 3 petals together. But leave both the halves of your holding cord (HC) A whole, since they will be used in assembly.

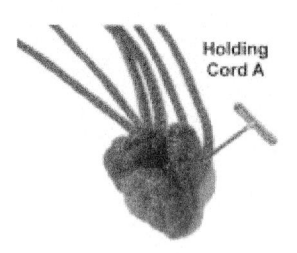

35. The intermediate petals for your Macramé Rose have more holding cords (HC) to select from. Locate holding cord six, which is next to your fifth working cord (WC), as well as your holding cord (HC) A. Preserve these cords whole. Cut off all the other working cords (WC) and the holding cords (HC). Melt the ends as you did in the last step and press them against the other ends. Now place the average petals right next to one another. Pass holding cord six from the left-hand petal underneath the one from the right side, and make a Double Half Hitch knot. Again apply glue before tightening the knot. Join them all in the same fashion, adding the first and last pettle. You can now cut off the holding cord (HC) 6 from every petal after the adhesive is entirely dried (optional).

Cord 6

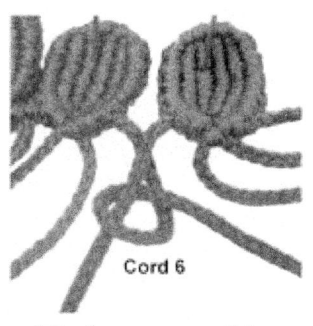

36. Repeat the step 33 for your big petals of the Macramé Rose. To join the petals, use holding cord (HC) 7, that is the 2nd holding cord (HC) below you're working cords (WC). Keep your holding cord (HC) A complete as well. Cut the other holding cords (HC) and the working cords (WC), finish them off at the ends by melting the stubs, and flattening them.
Connect the large 5 petals by taking cord 7 to make the Double Half Hitch. Apply a drop of adhesive before tightening the knot. When the glue dries, you can cut cord seven from every petal (optional).
37. Repeat the step 34 with the outermost petals, but do not trim off the cord seven after joining them. Keep these complete, along with holding cords (HC) A.
38. Place the cords that are left from the tiny petals through the circle or opening of your central petals. Then place these cords from the rings of your large petals. Now pass them from the outer petals.

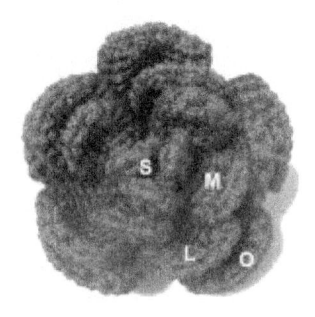

39. Assemble the petals in a manner so that they bend and are somewhat offset from each other, specifically the larger petals and the outermost petals.

    Make a Wrapped Knot (WK) at the end with the help of a two yard cord, Ensure it is tight. This is an optional step if you wish a different final method. Pull the cords tightly to ensure the petals are closely connected to each other. You can add floral tape to tie around the loose strings if you need a stem for the rose. Cut them at different lengths, this way they won't appear bulky.

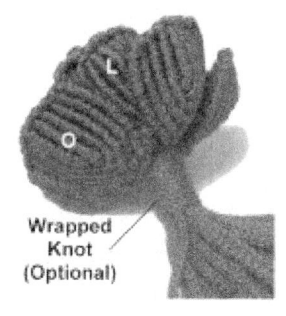

40. Another ending option is to cut off the excess cords two inches from the Wrapped Knot (WK) and untie to form a soft fuzzy ball.

4.2 DIY Macramé Feathers:

Once you get the hang of creating these feathers, they look so good and take almost no time to create.

Make them a single piece of art, or loop them from an unusual stick in your yard to make a boho wall hanging!

Materials Needed:

- Macramé Cord
- Stiffening Spray
- Sharp Scissors
- Tape Measure
- Wire Brush

Preparation:

Keep the cords sorted and divided by length. Cut the following cord lengths:

- **Big feather** – 1 – 24 inch piece, 10 – 12 inch pieces, 10 – 10 inch pieces, 10 – 8-inch pieces (31 total cords)
- **Small feathers** – 1 – 12" piece, 6 – 6 inch pieces, 4 – 4 inch pieces, 4 – 3 inch pieces (15 total cords)

If you look at a feather – it's marginally wider at the base and is skinnier at the top edges. So first, we begin with the longest cords, then go to our medium cords and finally finish with the shortest cords.

Step by Step Instruction:

1. Take the longest cord first and fold it halfway. This is the 24" piece, for the large feather. It is the 12" one, for the small feather. That long piece is our feather's "spine." Then, take and fold one of your longest cords in two. Place it perpendicular *to the right under* the spine of the feather, as seen in image # 1 below.

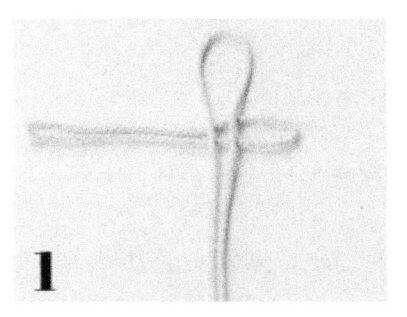

2. Take another of your cords, fold it in two. Drag the section of the rope through the first chord you've laid down (not the backbone). Drag it with the feather over the back.

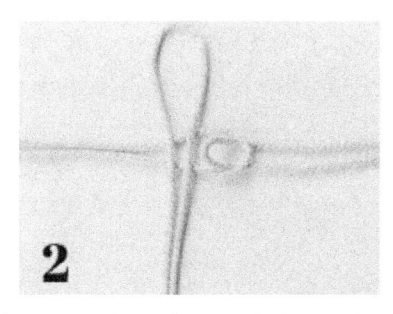

3. Take the first cord ends, and drag them into the second cords loop. You will have something close to image # 3 added below.

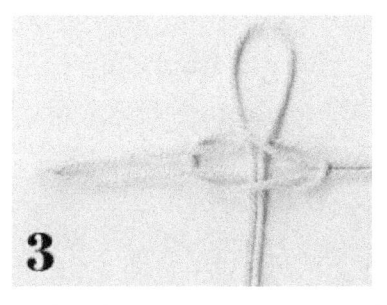

4. Push the cords close now! You made the first knot on the spine of your feather.

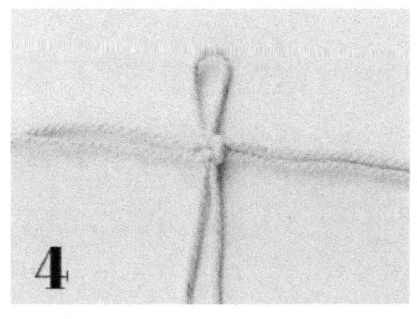

5. Then we will repeat phases 1-4, but we will switch directions. Take one of the longer strings,

and split in two. Place the loop (instead of the right) on the left side, as seen in image # 5.

6. Now take another string, fold it in half, and thread it right around the loop. Pull the ends up and then through this loop. For reference, see image # 6.

7. Pull each cord tightly and keep switching the sides -right, left, right, etc. When all of your longest cords are used, turn to the medium cords, using the same method. Switch to the smallest cords at the end.

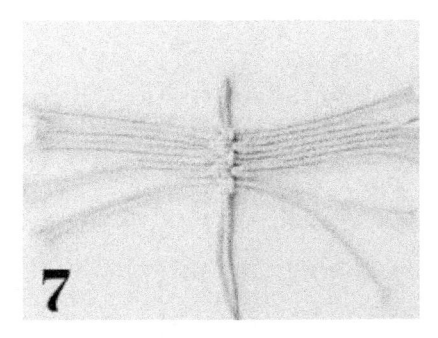

8. You will have something like in image # 8!

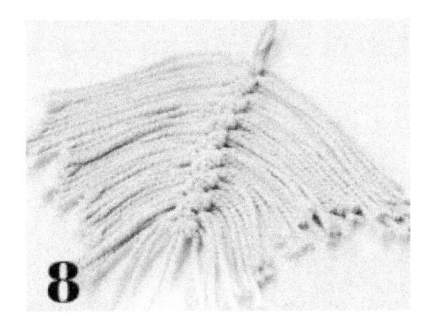

9. After all of your cords are used, you'll brush them out with a wire brush to create the strands. Hold the spine of the feather, so that no ties are pulled off accidentally.

Useful tip: *If you notice your spine still extending a lot, you should cut it up to balance it.*
You may undo the cords with your fingertips first. Or you can brush them off onto an old cloth so that no surfaces get damaged. But to get those good strands, you'll have to brush pretty fast!
Flip over the feather and brush both sides to ensure that the strings are all brushed off.

10. Take your scissors and cut your feather once you brush it all off.

    Spray the feather with a stiffening spray to make the feather stiffer so that it stays flat as it hangs.

    Follow this procedure to make the feathers bigger, or whatever size you choose!

11. These DIY Macramé feathers can be used for creating a lovely wall hanging too. Only take a dowel or stick and tie the stiffened feathers on it. However, a wall hanging won't work without stiffening them up, as the feathers would be too soft.

    You might even use them to create a fun framed photo. For this! Glue the feathers down to a piece of foam board or thick cardstock and frame them.

4.3 DIY Macramé Mason Jars

Once you've learned some basic or simple Macramé knots, then you're able to display your talents on a unique project.

This Macramé project is excellent for you since it uses standard mason jars (you may have a lot of this somewhere in your home). It needs simple Macramé knots-nothing complex.

This idea was influenced by these vases of rattan we all see everywhere now a days. They add a particular dimension to a typical ho-hum jar. A mason pots, in this case!

Mason pots are so useful! We can use them to store items in the pantry and other tiny things (such as dollars, sewing pins, or other little items). A set of elegant mason jars has something really homey about it.

Materials Needed:

- Macramé Cord-Any of your choice (with just one packet of rope you can create so many beautiful things)
- Mason Jars
- Scissors
- We will use one regular size jar and one bigger with a handle.

Preparation:

We will make two jars for this venture. One bigger-size mason pot with a handle and one normal-sized Mason jar.

On both jars,

We will cut the strings at the similar measurements – at the end, you'll have to take off the waste on the normal sized container. Having too much chord is always easier than getting too tiny!

The larger Mason jar has a pattern of one alternate square knot all the way around. You're going to use cords, each of which is six feet in length.

For the bigger jar, you'll need 6 cords, and the regular jar will require 8 cords.

The patterns

- Differ somewhat with each jar: the larger handled Mason jar (known in this lesson as Bigger): the design is one alternating square knot (ASK) all around the jar.
- Standard Mason pot (identified in this tutorial as Standard): The Design is two square knots (SK) followed by two alternating square knots (ASK) all the way around.

Step by Step Instruction:

1. Taking two of your six foot strings and loop them all around the jar's rim – tie them with a simple square knot (SK). Larger: Using one of your six foot

strings and tie them all around the jar's rim – with a standard knot securely.

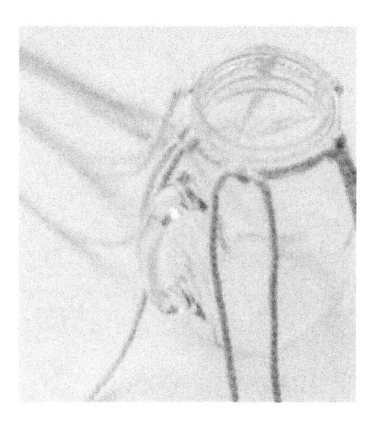

2. Attach remaining strings: Regular: take the remaining of your six strings and tie these to your pot using the reverse lark's head knots (RLHK). Bigger: Using the remainder of the five strings and fasten them to the container using the reverse lark's head knots. The ties must spread evenly along the jar's rim.

3. Make Square Knots (SK): Regular: create two rows of square knots (SK) all around the pot. Larger:

Make 1 row of alternating square knots around the container.

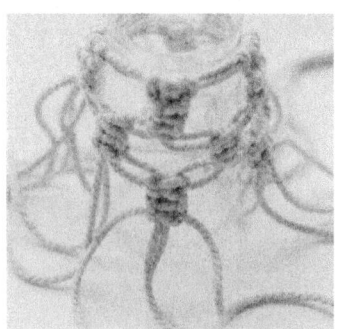

4. Move the design down the jar: Create a series of two alternating square knots (ASK) now. Continue on these alternating rows of square knots (SK) till you hit the lower end of the container. Larger: Start down the way with another series of alternating square knots (ASK). Do so until it reaches the jar's bottom.

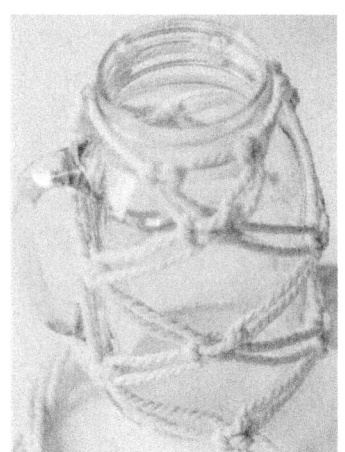

5. Complete the bottle: Regular / Larger: Cut off the extra rope before you hit the lower end of the pot, but keep it a little there and <u>comb</u> it for a fringe feel.

Chapter 5: Macramé Pattern: Fashion Item

5.1 Striped Clutch

This Clutch showcases picots with the sides of flap. A symmetrical stripe is created by using a 2nd color and switching between the right and left Square Knots. It is an extremely easy Macramé project, appropriate for a beginner. You must have some practice of tying Square Knots both left and right, but they are all explained as potion of the instructions. The dimensions of the finished clutch purse is 6.5 inches height (folded) and 9 inches wide. You can effortlessly create a broader version by adding more strings to it. Like the example illustrated, we are using two colors. A color is a brown, and B color is turquoise; you can use any color according to your preference.

Materials Needed:

- (50 yards) 4mm string material
- A small size button for the clasp
- Project board, some pins, glue, and tape

Knots Used:

- Barrel Knot (BK)

- Double Half Hitch (DHH)
- Alternating Square Knots (ASK)
- Square Knot (right and left both)

Preparation:
- Cut twenty cords of color A, each 4 yards in length.
- Cut extra strings into sets of two to keep the Clutch (striped) larger than 9 inches, make sure you have an even amount of strands.
- Cut four cords of color B, each 4 yards in length.

Step by Step Instructions:

1. Fold in half two of A color cords and tie them in the middle. The following picture shows you how to wrap a (Left Square) Knot at the flap edge to form the picots.
You can use these same set of details to produce all the left Square Knot used in creating the body of your Striped Clutch. Mentally mark the four parts, like they were four separate strings. For the left Square Knot, you always start by moving strand 1 towards the right, over filler cords 2 to 3 and under your working strand 4.
 Now move 4 cord to the left, under filler cords 2 to 3, and over the working string 1.

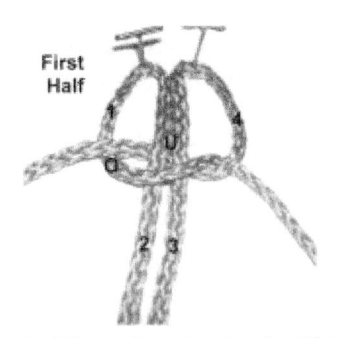

Shift the knot's first half so that it sits half-inch below the fold (for half-inch picot).

Cords 4 and 1 have changed places, and the position for the 2nd half of the SK is now reversed.

Pull cord 1 towards the left, over strings 2 to 3, and underneath cord 4. Pull cord 4 towards the right, underneath cords 2 - 3, and over cord 1.

2. Revise 1 step with two cords in color B, making 1 picot loop design.
3. The following guidelines are for the right Knot (SK) picot designs. Create at least seven picots with A color design. If you want the clutch that is striped to be broader than nine inches, you can make more picots in this color.
4. Create one picot with B color at the top.

For your right Square know, you begin by pulling 4 cord towards the left, over strings 2 to 3 and underneath strand 1. Now move strand 1 to the right, underneath strands 2 to 3, and over your working cord 4.

Move cord 4 to the right for the second half, over the filler cords 2-3 and underneath cord 1. Pull cord 1 towards the left, underneath cord 2-3, and over 4 cord.

5. Organize on the board all picot designs as follows: Three A colors Left picots (from steps 1 to 2), followed by one B color Left picot design created in step 3.
And one B color right picot created in step 4 that is follow by the 7 color A picot designs.

Any other picot designs that you've created needs to be placed on the right side of others.

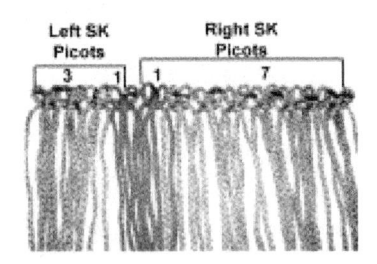

The Clutch that is striped is created using (ASK) Alternating Square Knots. Before beginning, you must know how to switch cords, so if you don't know about how pattern of ASK work, then practice. For each row, you will begin from the left, so the directions make sense. Mentally number all the cords from 1 - 48. Pay very clear focus on the direction of your Square Knot (left or right), as the stripe made with B color depends on the changes in direction.

Left SK: The working cords on the left hand side is moved first.
Right SK: First, working cords moved will be on the right.

6. The 1st row is tied in groups of 4, starting with cord 3.

The first 4 knots are left Square Knot made with the cords:

- 3 - 6 of color A
- 7 - 10 of color A
- 11 - 14 of color B and A combined
- 15 - 18 of color B

First Row of ASK

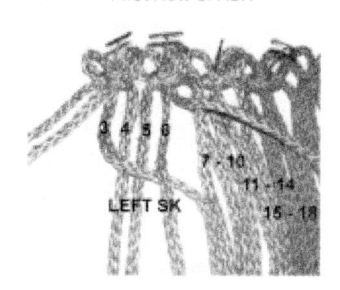

7. Now change to a right Square Knot when for which you are using cords 19 to 22, which is of color B and A combined. The knots remaining are all right Square Knots, of A color: Cords used are 27 - 30, 23 - 26, 35 - 38, 31 - 34, 39 - 42, and 43 - 46.

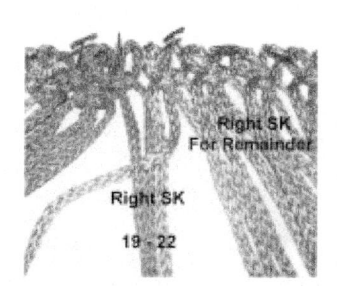

8. The 2nd of the row starts with the 4 remaining SK, tied with cords:

- 1 - 4 (A color)
- 5 - 8 (A color)
- 9 - 12 (A color)
- 13 - 16 (B color)

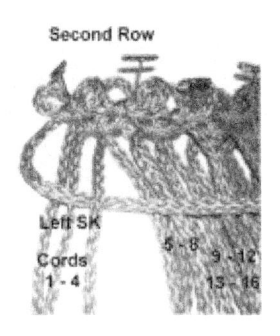

Second Row

9. Tie the 1st right square knot with cords 17 to 20, of color B.

The leftover loops are tied with the cords
21 to 24,
25 to 28,
29, 32,
33 to 36,
37 to 40,
41 to 44,
and 45 to 48.

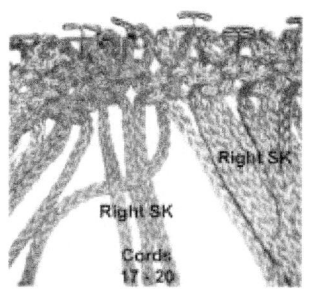

10. Redo 6th step but switch cords 2 & 3 before you do so. So the first left Square Knot is created with cords 2-4-5-6. Cord 2 is required to be used as a cord working only one time, and this is good spot to do it.

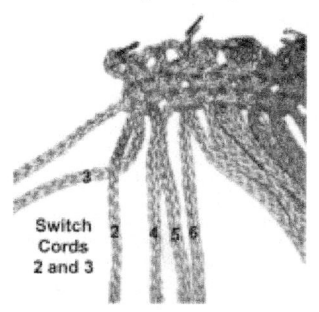

Repeat 7th step but switch cords 47 and 46 when you reach to the last ASK of that row. Now cords 43-44-45, and 47 will tie the final right Square Knot.

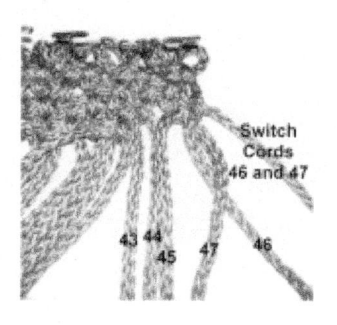

11. You repeat the steps 9 and 8 and then steps 7 and 6 for the rest of the striped clutch.

12. Repeat this step until the pattern is eighteen inches in length, from the top to the end row of ASK of the picots.
Stop on the row where cords 3 to 46 are used (steps 7 and 6).

Useful tip: Notice to make sure that the cords of color B are in the group always before starting each row. It's effortless to change cords around unintentionally, and that's BAD in this case. So be very careful while you are in the area that is striped, and pay clear attention towards the cord position (see the picture for reference).

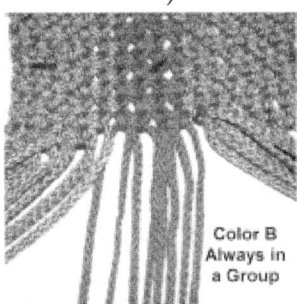

Color B Always in a Group

The two colors are blended on a stripe in the rows where the steps repeat 7 and 6. The Square knot is always started with the color A thread. For this situation, that is chord 11 since you're tying a left Square Knot.

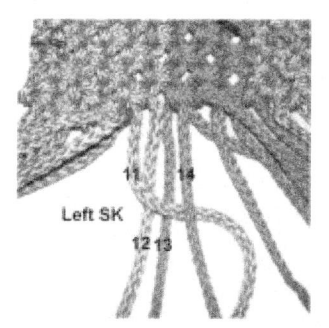

In this row, the next blended color knot also begins with the same working cord of color A. That's string 22 in this situation since you're creating a right Square Knot.

The last detail that you should observe is that the first 4 knots are all left Square Knots in each row, and the remainder are right SK's. Again, rightly changing directions at the right place is very important for creating this Striped Clutch. The lines won't be aligned otherwise.

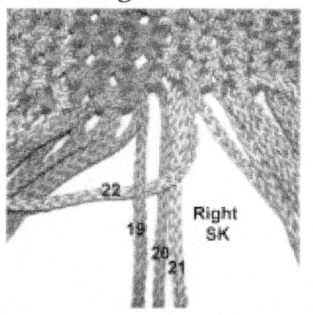

The Striped Clutch's front edge is made once all the ASK are attached or tied. Ensure that you have complete idea to tie a (DHH) Double Half Hitches.

13. Pull 1 cord to the right, and so it lies on above of all other string.

14. This cord will work as a holding or stopping cord for the first row of DHH's.

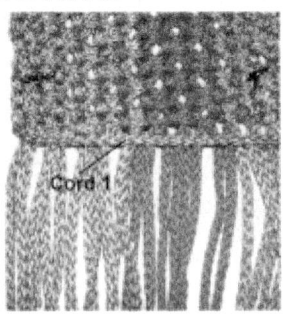

15. Connect cords 2 to 47 with DHH knot to holding 1 cord. While creating each loop, rotating counter clockwise. Securely tie each knot.

The formed bar should be placed against the last ASK row and bent a little to the right and left edges of the purse (just like in the next picture).

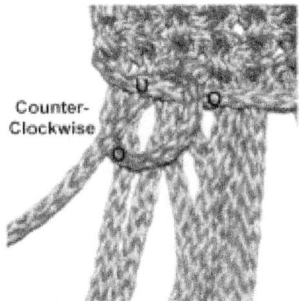

When you move forwards, push the ties as tight as you can to one another, so that you have space for all of the cords. Make sure that you don't connect cord 48 that is the last cord from the edge that is right to your Striped Clutch.

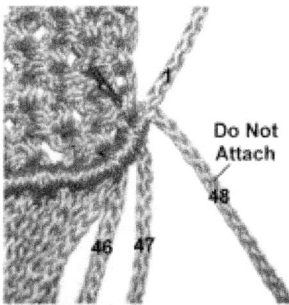

16. Now move cord 48 towards the left, located just below DHH's first section. Connect all the cords 47 to 2 in the same order with clockwise DHH knots. Once you got to the striped area, stop there.

17. End the strings by cutting them down to two inches each. Flip the clutch that is striped, so you are now working with the back. Slide single cord through the loop created under 1 row, which is the row underneath the ASK row. Use tweezers and pliers if needed for this step.

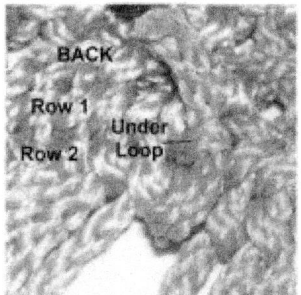

This clutch must be lined, hiding the cut corners of the cords. If you don't want to do this, cut the cords a bit more, and add glue to stick them to the inside layer. You should burn (heat) the tips with a fire if using synthetic materials like nylon, to melt the substance at the edges to avoid the fray.

18. Now it's safe to lace the slides up to the clutch. Begin by taking measurement of the clutch down to five inches, starting from the picots. That is the flap of your clutch, so fold it here. Pull down 6 and half inches and again fold it. This will separate the back to the front end. The section with the DHH knots is your front. Grip the bag between your thighs, or place it on one corner. There are knots in between the rows of Alternating Square Knot along the sides of the clutch. Line up the knots at the back and front sections so they are in direct to each other. There will be a single knot at the fold in the front and the back. Use two 18 "scrap cord pieces, or two new pieces, to tie the edges.

Slip your lacing cord in the end rows of DHH's make sure you are as near to the edge as feasible from the front of the clutch. Now slide it straight across a loop from the back of the clutch.

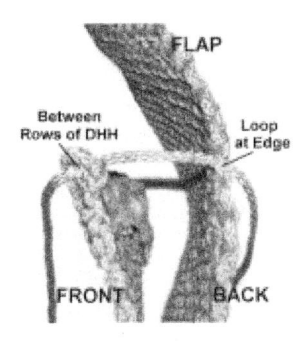

19. Make a cross using the two ends of your lacing cord's, and then move them into the loops of next set. Move them from in to outside.

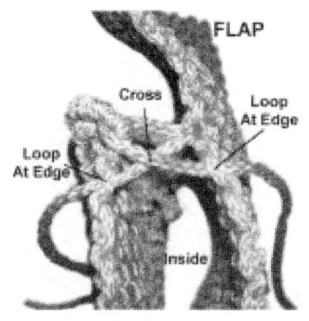

20. Redo 18th step several times more, bypassing the ends from another loops, till you meet the flipped (folded) area in the front and the back. Once you reach the fold, move both your ends from the similar loop, bringing them to the inner side of your Striped Clutch. Before you go on, ensure the lacing is firm.

Pass Both Ends Through One Loop

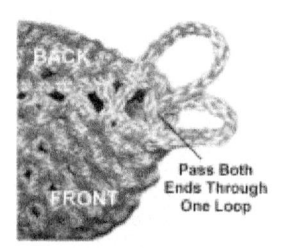

BACK / FRONT

21. Turn the clutch inside out, so that the lacing string is on the outer side and easier to handle. Hold a Barrel Knot (Extra Loop and Overhand Knot) to hold it in place. Trim off the excess material near the knot, then add a little glue to it. When you are using a synthetic material cord, you can melt the material with the fire. Flip the clutch that is striped inside out, so that the edges that are cut are on the inner side.

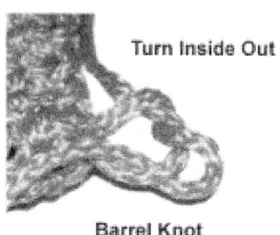

Turn Inside Out

Barrel Knot

22. You can add a lining into it right around the ends. The good area to stitch it in the forward area is inside the (two) rows of DHH. There's enough area for a thread and needle.

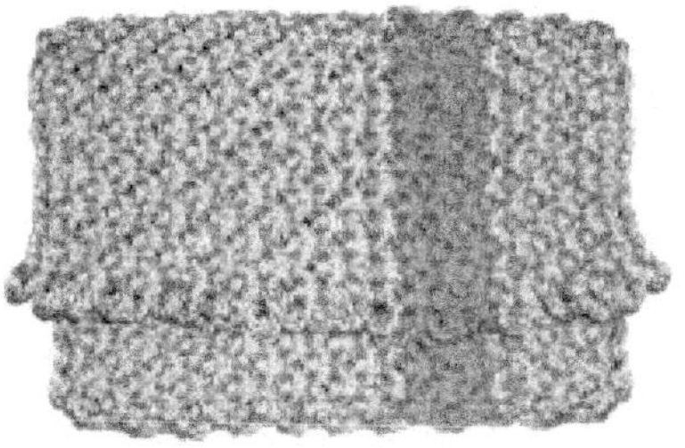

Conclusion

For all the Macramé beginners who may have stumbled upon this book by chance, welcome! This book is written in honor of your spirit, to delve into the experience of knotting despite its lack of demand. A tiny community around the globe still practice macramé. Most of these people are mature and older and may have learned the art of Macramé during its heyday in the '70s.

Macramé has been embraced as a versatile, potential, trendy craft worthy of complementing other fashionable products for the expansion in the process of product development, which has a culture and economic interests as well as a sustaining culture. Some of the assumptions that have been drawn are that macramé craft has become a whole feature of our traditional arts, especially among the youth, and is still experiencing increasingly notable change.

Now the art of Macramé is reviving. Because of its use in jewelry that has been making the rounds in the fashion industry. The same decorative patterns are seen in elegant clothes, purses, caps, and belts.

Macramé is a way to create textiles that use knots rather than other techniques of weaving or knitting. Macramé was initially used by sailors to decorate artifacts or their ships, but now it is often used to make shoes, containers, sheets, hangers for plants, and other things like wall hangings for walls.

In Victorian ara, Macramé was remarkably popular as a lacework and was used for decorations on everything from jackets to underclothing, curtains, ornaments and jewelry. During the 70's it made another comeback, using the kind of jute plant holders and Macramé bird wall hangers.

Macramé has become popular once again, and today is seen in the form of Macramé jewelry, clothing, and accessories. Beginners and seasoned pros alike will find this book to be a great source of knowledge and inspiration for patterns and new ideas. If you are learning how to Macramé or you've been at it for years, you will find lots of great information.

In this book you will learn some common words, abbreviations, and methods used in macramé instructions for creating different designs or patterns. You may also learn about different kinds of materials used for macramé. There are several recognized fabrics used to do macramé. These include silk, rayon, raffia threads, shoe sewing threads, cotton threads, jute, cloth strips, leather strips, shoelace, and all other lightweights, malleable, foldable, durable and hand safe fabrics.

Yet jute, silk, linen, and cotton are the most common fabrics used for Macramé as they tie easily, come in several sizes, can be dyed, and are readily available. Leather and suede are also sometimes used for macramé.

You will learn about a wide variety of knots and knots combinations that are found in macramé, including the square knot, a half knot, half hitch, and the larks head knot. You can learn various patterns which can be created depending on the knots used and ether they are used individually or in addition to others. Some ordinary bags, and also the friendship bracelets created by many kids, are made with macramé as well.

This book also features a vied range of patterns ranging from essential pieces like decorative ornaments and key chains to more complex ones like bags, belts, and baskets. This book is an excellent guide for both fresher and experienced knitters.

Printed in Great Britain
by Amazon